Clavimate Presents

TAKE CHARGE
of your
HABITS

A Practical Guide to Transforming Your
Habits for Success

WRITTEN BY
DR. SURAJ KUMAR NAYAK

NewDelhi • London

BLUEROSE PUBLISHERS
India | U.K.

Copyright © Dr. Suraj Kumar Nayak 2024

All rights reserved by author. No part of this publication may be reproduced, stored in a retrieval system or transmitted in any form or by any means, electronic, mechanical, photocopying, recording or otherwise, without the prior permission of the author. Although every precaution has been taken to verify the accuracy of the information contained herein, the publisher assumes no responsibility for any errors or omissions. No liability is assumed for damages that may result from the use of information contained within.

BlueRose Publishers takes no responsibility for any damages, losses, or liabilities that may arise from the use or misuse of the information, products, or services provided in this publication.

For permissions requests or inquiries regarding this publication,
please contact:

BLUEROSE PUBLISHERS
www.BlueRoseONE.com
info@bluerosepublishers.com
+91 8882 898 898
+4407342408967

ISBN: 978-93-6783-539-5

Cover design: Shubham
Typesetting: Sagar

First Edition: November 2024

Dedication

This Book is dedicated to **Dipti Ranjan Patnaik** *sir, whose belief in me remained steadfast when the entire world, except my family, could not support the continuation of my research on habit transformation. Dipti Ranjan Patnaik, a visionary industrialist from Odisha, is renowned for his leadership in mining, power, and hospitality. An NIT Rourkela alumnus, he champions sustainable growth, education, and cultural preservation. With ventures like Atmosphere Hospitality, he blends innovation with social impact.*

This book is my first humble offering at his lotus feet, as I have felt the divine transformation of my life through his unwavering support and mentorship.

Thank you, sir, for being the guiding force that helped me realize this dream.

— **Dr. Suraj Kumar Nayak**

Preface

Take Charge of Your Habits: Creating an Unbreakable Achievers Mindset and Growth Journey

In a world filled with distractions and challenges, the difference between those who simply survive and those who truly thrive lies in the mastery of one powerful force: habits. The habits we form shape our lives, guide our daily actions, and determine the trajectory of our future. This book, Take Charge of Your Habits, is not just another self-help manual; it is a transformational guide designed to help you build an Unbreakable Achievers Mindset and set yourself on a growth journey like no other.

This book is structured around "missions," each of which is a milestone that focuses on developing crucial aspects of habit transformation, self-discipline, resilience, and growth. Every mission is an opportunity to cultivate the kind of habits that successful individuals embody. These habits—whether in time management, productivity, self-reflection, or continuous learning—are the building blocks of greatness. And greatness, in itself, is not an outcome but a series of daily practices, small decisions, and consistent actions that lead to profound results.

Why This Book?

Many people set goals with enthusiasm, only to find themselves lost or demotivated along the way. This happens because they lack the right habits and systems to support sustained effort and growth. By guiding you through a series of carefully curated missions, this book serves as a step-by-step blueprint to help you rewire your habits for success. Each mission is filled with actionable steps that are designed to be challenging yet achievable, pushing you out of your comfort zone while also providing the support you need to succeed.

Building the Unbreakable Achievers Mindset

An Unbreakable Achiever's Mindset is about more than just reaching goals; it's about developing a mental framework that empowers you to face any challenge with confidence, perseverance, and creativity. This mindset is not innate but can be cultivated by anyone willing to put in the effort. The key lies in adopting and mastering the habits that drive growth, foster resilience, and create a powerful, unstoppable momentum.

The missions outlined in this book are designed to help you not only achieve your immediate goals but also establish a foundation for lifelong success and fulfilment. Each mission focuses on a different aspect of growth—whether it's improving your focus, enhancing your time management skills, or fostering deeper self-awareness. By committing to these missions, you are setting yourself up for a lifetime of achievement and personal evolution.

Completing the Journey: Embracing Growth and Transformation

The path to creating an Unbreakable Achievers Mindset is not a linear one; it requires persistence, self-compassion, and a willingness to embrace failure as a part of the learning process. Growth happens not in the absence of obstacles but in the mastery of overcoming them. The more you invest in this journey, the more you will see how each mission, step, and action contributes to your overall transformation.

This book is a call to action. It challenges you to step up, take control of your habits, and build a future that you are truly proud of. As you embark on this journey, remember that every milestone you reach is a testament to your commitment to growth. With each completed mission, you will see not only changes in your habits but also in your mindset, confidence, and the impact you have on the world around you.

A Final Note to the Learner

Every great journey starts with a single step. Let this book be the beginning of your journey to becoming the best version of yourself. As you work through each mission, you will find that growth is not just about achieving but about becoming—becoming more resilient, more focused, and more aligned with your true potential.

Believe in yourself, embrace the process, and, most importantly, take charge of your habits. The journey to an Unbreakable Achievers Mindset starts here.

Are you ready to embark on this transformative journey? The first mission awaits you.

— **Dr. Suraj Kumar Nayak**

Contents

Chapter – 1 1
    1.1. Mission 1 Day 1: Introduction to Habit Awareness 1
    1.2. Mission 1 Day 2: Understanding the Habit Loop 11
    1.3. Mission 1 Day 3: Identifying and Managing Cues and Triggers 18
    1.4. Mission 1 Day 4: Routines: Building the Right Actions 26
    1.5. Mission 1 Day 5: Rewards: Reinforcing Positive Habits 41
    1.6. Mission 1 Day 6: Habit Tracking: Monitoring Progress 51
    1.7. Mission 1 Day 7: Reviewing and Adjusting Your Habits 62

Chapter – 2 73
    2.1. Mission 2 Day 1: Overcoming Obstacles 73
    2.2. Mission 2 Day 2: Staying Motivated 81
    2.3. Mission 2 Day 3: Resilience Building 87
    2.4. Mission 2 Day 4: Consistency Planning 94
    2.5. Mission 2 Day 5: Accountability 102
    2.6. Mission 2 Day 6: Habit Stacking 109
    2.7. Mission 2 Day 7: Mission 2 Reflection 116

Chapter – 3 124
    3.1. Mission 3 Day 1: Deepening Your Understanding of Cues 124
    3.2. Mission 3 Day 2: Optimizing Routine Design 130
    3.3. Mission 3 Day 3: Maximizing Rewards for Habit Reinforcement 135
    3.4. Mission 3 Day 4: Advanced Habit Tracking Techniques 140
    3.5. Mission 3 Day 5: Building Habit Streaks 145
    3.6. Mission 3 Day 6: Overcoming Streak Breaks 151
    3.7. Mission 3 Day 7: Mission 3 Reflection 156

Chapter – 4 162
    4.1. Mission 4 Day 1: Habit Automation 162
    4.2. Mission 4 Day 2: Reframing - Changing Your Perspective 169

4.3. Mission 4 Day 3: Habit Chains - Linking Multiple Habits for Efficiency . 173
4.4. Mission 4 Day 4: Environmental Design 179
4.5. Mission 4 Day 5: Behavioural Sustitution 183
4.6. Mission 4 Day 6: Reinforcement Systems... 189
4.7. Mission 4 Day 7: Review and Reflect - Mission 4 Wrap-Up.................... 199

Chapter – 5 208
5.1. Mission 5 Day 1: Understanding Your Unique Habit Profile 208
5.2. Mission 5 Day 2: Tailoring habit Techniques to Your Personality 215
5.3. Mission 5 Day 3: Building a Personalized Habit Toolkit......................... 221
5.4. Mission 5 Day 4: Overcoming Personal Challenges in Habit Formation .. 208
5.5. Mission 5 Day 5: Leveraging Strengths and Addressing Weaknesses 235
5.6. Mission 5 Day 6: Creating a Customized Habit Plan............................... 241
5.7. Mission 5 Day 7: Reflection and Next Steps 247

Chapter – 6 252
6.1. Mission 6 Day 1: Habit Mastery and Beyond... 252
6.2. Mission 6 Day 2: Advanced Habit Stacking Techniques 258
6.3. Mission 6 Day 3: Building a Resilient Exercise Habit 6.3.1. Theory: 263
6.4. Mission 6 Day 4: Long-Term Habit Sustainability 271
6.5. Mission 6 Day 5: Adapting Habits to Life Changes 277
6.6. Mission 6 Day 6: Expanding Your Habit Repertoire 282
6.7. Mission 6 Day 7: Reflection and Recap - Habit Mastery Journey............. 288

Appendix: Additional Resources for Helping Students in Self-study 293
Mission Daily Check-In Template... 294
Weekly Reflection After a Test/Mission to Improve Next Time 299
Weekly Productivity Plan 302
Daily Habit Tracker 303

Chapter – 1

1.1. Mission 1 Day 1: Introduction to Habit Awareness

1.1.1. Theory

Habits are foundational to personal development, driving up to 40% of our daily actions. They shape our lives, impacting health, productivity, and overall well-being. By understanding the process of habit formation, we can harness their power to make meaningful changes.

What is a Habit?

- A habit is a routine behaviour repeated regularly, often occurring subconsciously. It's ingrained in our daily routine.
    - **Example:** Brushing your teeth every morning is a habit performed without thinking.

Recognizing that habits guide much of our daily behaviour allows us to leverage them for positive change.

How Habits Are Formed

- Habits form through the **Habit Loop:** Cue → Routine → Reward. This loop repeats until the behaviour becomes automatic.

It begins with a cue (trigger), followed by a routine (the behaviour), and ends with a reward (reinforcing the habit). Repetition of this loop strengthens the habit.

The Science Behind Habits

- **Habits are formed in the basal ganglia**, a part of the brain responsible for routine behaviours.
- **Repetition strengthens neural pathways**, making the habit more automatic over time. The more we practice a behaviour, the easier it becomes.
- **Image Suggestion:** An illustration of the brain highlighting the basal ganglia.

Types of Habits

- **Keystone Habits:** Small changes that trigger positive effects in other areas of life (e.g., regular exercise leading to better diet choices).
- **Atomic Habits:** Small, incremental habits that compound over time, leading to significant results (e.g., reading one page daily).

Why it matters?

Understanding your habits is the first step to taking control of your life. Awareness helps you identify which behaviors are supporting or sabotaging your goals. By recognizing automatic patterns, you gain the power to replace detrimental habits with positive ones. Habit awareness fosters self-discipline and aligns your actions with your long-term aspirations. It creates clarity, allowing you to focus on what truly matters. This understanding is a foundation for growth, as habits shape nearly every aspect of your health, productivity, and relationships. Embracing awareness means taking the driver's seat in your personal development journey.

Inspiring Thoughts to Reflect On

Aristotle was an ancient Greek philosopher and student of Plato, who profoundly influenced Western thought in areas like ethics, logic, and science. Known for his belief in cultivating virtues through consistent action, Aristotle said once —

"We are what we repeatedly do. Excellence, then, is not an act, but a habit."

For more resources, follow step-by-step:

- Scan the QR-code
- Register/Login Using Email-Id or Phone No.
- Browse through course videos
- Access Feeds for daily motivational & tricks for habit transformation

1.1.2. Mission 1 Day 1 Worksheet:

Instructions: Take some time to observe your daily routines and habits. This worksheet will help you identify the habits you currently have and assess whether they are beneficial or detrimental to your goals.

Worksheet Sections:

Section 1: Identifying Current Habits

Morning Routine:

- What do you do as soon as you wake up? (e.g., check your phone, brush your teeth, exercise)

  _____
  _____
  _____

- Are these habits helping you start your day positively?

  _____
  _____

Work/Study Habits:

- What habits guide you during work, personal projects, or leisure time? (e.g., taking frequent breaks, staying focused)

  _____
  _____
  _____
  _____

- How do these habits impact your productivity?

  _____
  _____

_____
_____
_____

Evening Routine:
- How do you wind down at the end of the day?

_____
_____
_____
_____

- Are these habits conducive to a good night's sleep?

_____
_____
_____

Section 2: Assessing Your Habits

Positive Habits:
- List the habits that you believe are beneficial to your health, productivity, and well-being.

_____
_____
_____
_____
_____
_____

- How can you reinforce these habits?

_____
_____
_____
_____
_____

Negative Habits:
- List the habits that you believe are detrimental to your goals.

_____
_____
_____
_____

- What triggers these habits, and how can you start changing them?

_____
_____
_____
_____

Section 3: Action Plan

Choose One Habit to Focus On:
- Identify one habit you want to change or develop.

_____
_____
_____
_____

_____

_____

- Describe the steps you will take to work on this habit over the next Mission.

_____

_____

_____

_____

_____

_____

For more resources, follow step-by-step:

- Scan the QR-code
- Register/Login Using Email-Id or Phone No.
- Browse through course videos
- Access Feeds for daily motivational & tricks for habit transformation

1.1.3. Sample filled-up Worksheet for a Disciplined Person:

Section 1: Identifying Current Habits

Morning Routine:
- What do you do as soon as you wake up?

I wake up at 6:00 AM, drink a glass of water, do a quick stretching exercise, go to a 45 minutes long morning walk, and then review my to-do list for the day before starting my work.

- Are these habits helping you start your day positively?

Yes, they help me feel energized and focused from the start of the day.

Work/Study Habits:
- What habits do you have while working or studying?

I usually start by prioritizing my tasks, working in 50-minute focused sessions with 10-minute breaks, and reviewing my work in regular gaps. I also avoid distractions by keeping my phone in silent mode during the session.

- How do these habits impact your productivity?

These habits help me maintain high productivity and ensure that I understand and retain the material effectively.

Evening Routine:
- How do you wind down at the end of the day?

I review my progress for the day, plan the next day, and spend some time reading or doing something relaxing, like playing basketball or listening to favourite music.

- Are these habits conducive to a good night's sleep?

Yes, they help me clear my mind and ensure I get enough rest, which is crucial for staying alert and productive. I have noticed that I sleep well due to these habit patterns I have.

Section 2: Assessing Your Habits

Positive Habits:

- List the habits that you believe are beneficial to your health, productivity, and well-*being.*
    - Regular exercise/gym in the morning.
    - Consistent work schedule with focused sessions.
    - Reviewing and planning my tasks daily.
    - Taking breaks to stay refreshed and avoid burnout.
- How can you reinforce these habits?

I can reinforce these habits by setting mission-based goals, rewarding myself for sticking to my routine and reflecting on what works well so I can continue improving.

Negative Habits:

- List the habits that you believe are detrimental to your goals.
    - Sometimes, I overwork myself and don't take enough breaks.
    - Occasionally, I focus too much on perfection, which slows me down.
- What triggers these habits, and how can you start changing them?

Overworking is triggered by the pressure to perform well. I can start by reminding myself that balance is key and that taking breaks will actually improve my productivity. I'll focus more on progress rather than perfection.

Section 3: Action Plan

- **Choose One Habit to Focus On:**

Maintaining a healthy balance between work and rest.

- **Describe the steps you will take to work on this habit over the next Mission:**

1. Schedule regular breaks in my daily routine to ensure I stay refreshed.

2. Set a strict cut-off time for personal work in the evening to allow for relaxation before bed.

4. Reflect on my energy levels daily to ensure I'm not overworking myself.

1.1.4. Sample filled-up Worksheet for a Struggling Person:

Section 1:

Morning Routine:

- What do you do as soon as you wake up?

I often check emails first thing and sometimes spend too much time scrolling.

- **Are these habits helping you start your day positively?**

Checking emails immediately adds stress before I fully wake up. I want to feel more refreshed before starting work tasks.

Work/Study Habits:

- **What habits guide you during work, personal projects, or leisure time?**

I often try to respond to emails as they come, which disrupts my focus. I also tend to work without breaks until I'm tired.

- **How do these habits impact your productivity?**

Constant email-checking lowers my focus, and working without breaks drains my energy by mid-day.

Evening Routine:

- **How do you wind down at the end of the day?**

I usually watch TV late into the evening, which sometimes makes it hard to fall asleep quickly.

- **Are these habits conducive to a good night's sleep?**

Not really, as screen time keeps me awake longer than I'd like.

Section 2: Assessing Your Habits

Positive Habits:

- **List the habits that you believe are beneficial to your health, productivity, and well-being.**

When I manage to take short breaks during work, I feel refreshed. Morning stretching also helps me feel ready for the day.

- **How can you reinforce these habits?**

Set reminders to take breaks and keep exercise clothes by my bed as a morning prompt.

Negative Habits:

- **List the habits that you believe are detrimental to your goals.**

Checking emails first thing in the morning and watching TV late at night.

- **What triggers these habits, and how can you start changing them?**

I check emails out of habit and because I worry about missing something urgent. To change, I could dedicate a set time later in the morning for emails and set a reminder to turn off the TV earlier.

Section 3: Action Plan

Choose One Habit to Focus On:

- **Identify one habit you want to change or develop.**

I want to change my habit of checking emails first thing in the morning.

- **Describe the steps you will take to work on this habit over the next Mission.**

I will delay email-checking until after I have a morning stretch and coffee. I'll also set my phone to 'Do Not Disturb' until a specific time each morning to avoid the temptation.

For more resources, follow step-by-step:

- Scan the QR-code
- Register/Login Using Email-Id or Phone No.
- Browse through course videos
- Access Feeds for daily motivational & tricks for habit transformation

1.2. Mission 1 Day 2: Understanding the Habit Loop

1.2.1. Theory

The Habit Loop is the fundamental cycle that creates and sustains habits. It consists of three key components: Cue, Routine, and Reward. Recognizing and understanding this loop is essential for habit change and building new, positive behaviours.

What is the Habit Loop?

- The Habit Loop consists of:
  - **Cue:** The trigger that initiates the habit.
  - **Routine:** The behaviour or action that follows the cue.
  - **Reward:** The benefit gained from the routine, reinforcing the habit.
- **Example:** Feeling tired (Cue) prompts you to grab a coffee (Routine) to feel energized (Reward). This loop repeats until the behaviour becomes automatic.

Over time, this loop becomes automatic, requiring little conscious thought. Your brain starts craving the reward whenever the cue appears, solidifying the habit.

Identifying Your Habit Loops

- **Pay Attention to Cues:** Notice what triggers your habits—time, location, emotions, or specific situations.
- **Observe Your Routines:** Identify the actions you take in response to these cues.
- **Identify the Rewards:** Recognize what rewards reinforce these routines, driving the habit loop.

Understanding your current habit loops is the first step in altering or building new habits.

- **Breaking and Building Habit Loops**
- **Breaking:** To disrupt a negative habit loop, change the routine in response to the same cue and experiment with different rewards. For example, instead of snacking when stressed (Cue), try taking a short walk (New Routine) to achieve relaxation (Reward).

- **Building New Loops:** Choose a simple cue, design an easy routine, and select a rewarding outcome to motivate repetition. For instance, feeling stressed (Cue) triggers a 5-minute walk (Routine), leading to calmness (Reward).

Why it matters?

The habit loop (cue, routine, and reward) is the key to understanding how habits form and stick. Recognizing this cycle empowers you to modify existing habits or create new ones effectively. This knowledge helps break unproductive patterns and ensures consistency in positive behaviors. By mastering the habit loop, you gain the tools to rewire your brain, making personal growth more sustainable. It transforms conscious effort into automatic success, ensuring long-term improvements in areas like health, career, and relationships. Understanding this framework is vital for those seeking to turn aspirations into achievable, lasting habits.

Inspiring Thoughts to Reflect On

Robert Collier was a self-help author and advertising innovator who emphasized the power of persistence and incremental effort to achieve success. He said —

"Success is the sum of small efforts repeated day in and day out."

For more resources, follow step-by-step:
- Scan the QR-code
- Register/Login Using Email-Id or Phone No.
- Browse through course videos
- Access Feeds for daily motivational & tricks for habit transformation

1.2.2. Mission 1 Day 2 Worksheet:

Instructions: Use this worksheet to analyze your own habit loops. Identify the cues, routines, and rewards in your daily habits to better understand how they operate.

Worksheet Sections:

Section 1: Identify a Habit Loop

- **Habit:** Describe a habit you have.
  _____

- **Cue:** What triggers this habit? (e.g., time of day, emotion, location)
  _____

- **Routine:** What action do you take when the cue appears?
  _____
  _____

- **Reward:** What do you gain from this routine? (e.g., relief, pleasure, satisfaction)
  _____
  _____

Section 2: Analyzing the Habit Loop

- **Positive or Negative Habit:** Is this habit beneficial or harmful to your goals?
  _____
  _____

- **Modify the Routine:** What alternative routine could you implement when the cue appears?

  _____
  _____
  _____

- **Experiment with Rewards:** What new reward could reinforce this new routine?

  _____
  _____
  _____

Section 3: Action Plan

- **New Habit Loop:** Describe the new habit loop you want to create.

Cue: _____

Routine: _____

Reward: _____

- **Commitment:** How will you remind yourself to practice this new habit loop?

  _____
  _____
  _____

1.2.3. Sample filled-up Worksheet for a Disciplined Person:

Section 1: Identify a Habit Loop

- **Habit:** Reviewing emails at the start of the workday to ensure everything is on track.
- **Cue:** Starting the workday and sitting down at the desk.
- **Routine:** I immediately open my inbox, check for urgent tasks, and sort emails.
- **Reward:** A sense of preparedness and confidence, knowing the day's priorities are clear.

Section 2: Analyzing the Habit Loop

- **Positive or Negative Habit:** This habit is positive for productivity, but it can sometimes set a rushed tone if the inbox is overwhelming.
- **Modify the Routine:** Instead of diving into emails, I could start with a 5-minute planning session to outline goals before checking emails.
- **Experiment with Rewards:** I could reward myself with a brief coffee break or quiet reflection time to reinforce the benefits of a calm start.

Section 3: Action Plan
New Habit Loop:

- **Cue:** Sitting down at the desk.
- **Routine:** Spend five minutes setting daily priorities before opening emails.
- **Reward:** A relaxed start to the day, followed by a rewarding coffee break.
- **Commitment:** I will set a daily calendar reminder to plan before checking emails. I'll also leave a note on my desk as a visual cue.

Commitment:

I will maintain a study journal to track my progress and the effectiveness of active recall techniques. I will also set a daily alarm as a reminder to stick to this routine and periodically assess my academic performance to ensure this habit remains beneficial.

1.2.4. Sample filled-up Worksheet for a Struggling Person:

Instructions: Use this worksheet to analyze your own habit loops. Identify the cues, routines, and rewards in your daily habits to better understand how they operate.

Section 1: Identify a Habit Loop

- **Habit:** Procrastinating on assignments.
- **Cue:** Feeling overwhelmed by the amount of work, usually in the evening when I realize how much I still need to do.
- **Routine:** I avoid starting the assignment and instead distract myself with social media or watching videos.
- **Reward:** Temporary relief from stress and anxiety, as well as a false sense of comfort by avoiding the task.

Section 2: Analyzing the Habit Loop

- **Positive or Negative Habit:** This habit is negative because it prevents me from achieving my academic goals and leads to last-minute stress.
- **Modify the Routine:** Instead of avoiding the assignment, I could break the task into smaller, more manageable parts and start with a quick, easy section to build momentum.
- **Experiment with Rewards:** Reward myself with a short break or a treat after completing each small part of the assignment. This could reinforce the new routine of starting work immediately when I feel overwhelmed.

Section 3: Action Plan

New Habit Loop:

- **Cue:** Feeling overwhelmed in the evening.
- **Routine:** Break the assignment into smaller tasks and start working on the easiest part first.
- **Reward:** Take a 10-minute break or enjoy a small treat after completing a section.

Commitment:

I will set reminders on my phone and post a note on my study desk to prompt me to start with small tasks and reward myself after completion. Additionally, I will check in with an accountability partner daily to track my progress.

For more resources, follow step-by-step:

- Scan the QR-code
- Register/Login Using Email-Id or Phone No.
- Browse through course videos
- Access Feeds for daily motivational & tricks for habit transformation

1.3. Mission 1 Day 3: Identifying and Managing Cues and Triggers

1.3.1. Theory

Cues are the signals or events that trigger a habit. They act as the starting point for the Habit Loop, prompting us to take certain actions. By identifying and managing cues, you can gain greater control over your habits and make lasting changes. As an example, the sound of your alarm (cue) prompts you to get out of bed and start your morning routine.

Common Types of Cues

- **Time-Based Cues:** Specific times of day, such as morning, lunchtime, or bedtime, often serve as triggers for habits.
- **Location-Based Cues:** Physical places can trigger habits. Entering a gym might automatically make you want to exercise.
- **Emotional Cues:** Feelings like stress, boredom, or happiness can drive behaviours. Feeling stressed might trigger the habit of snacking.
- **Social Cues:** Being around certain people or in specific social settings can prompt habits, such as drinking coffee when meeting a friend.
- **Environmental Cues:** Visual or auditory signals in your surroundings, like seeing a food commercial, can induce cravings and actions.

Identifying Your Cues

- **Observe Your Habits:** Pay attention to your daily habits and note what triggers them. Keep an eye out for patterns in behaviour.
- **Keep a Journal:** Record times, locations, emotions, and other factors that coincide with your habits.
- **Reflect on Social and Environmental Influences:** Notice how people around you and your environment affect your behaviours.

Managing Cues

- **Avoid Negative Cues:** Change your environment to remove or avoid cues that trigger unwanted habits.

- **Create Positive Cues:** Set up cues that encourage good habits. Placing a water bottle on your desk can prompt you to drink more water throughout the day.
- **Use Reminders:** Set alarms or place visual reminders around your space to reinforce new habits.

Why it matters?

Cues and triggers are the starting points for all habits. By identifying what prompts your behaviors, you can take control of automatic actions and redirect them toward positive outcomes. Recognizing and managing triggers gives you the power to design your environment and mindset for success. This awareness is crucial for breaking bad habits and forming new ones, as it allows you to disrupt harmful patterns and replace them with beneficial routines. Mastering this step empowers you to create a life aligned with your goals, one habit at a time.

Inspiring Thoughts to Reflect On

Charles Duhigg, author of The *Power of Habit*, has discussed how recognizing and reshaping triggers is essential to habit change, empowering people to take control of their behaviors and achieve lasting transformation. As an unknown person said —

"Triggers are not destiny—they are opportunities to take control and change your path."

For more resources, follow step-by-step:

- Scan the QR-code
- Register/Login Using Email-Id or Phone No.
- Browse through course videos
- Access Feeds for daily motivational & tricks for habit transformation

1.3.2. Mission 1 Day 3 Worksheet:

Instructions: Use this worksheet to identify the cues that trigger your habits. This will help you understand what drives your behaviour and how you can manage these cues to change your habits.

Workout Sections:

Section 1: Identifying Cues

- **Habit:** Describe a habit you want to analyze.

  _____
  _____

- **Time-Based Cues:** When does this habit typically occur?

  _____
  _____

- **Location-Based Cues:** Where are you when this habit happens?

  _____
  _____

- **Emotional Cues:** What emotions do you feel when this habit occurs?

  _____
  _____
  _____

- **Social Cues:** Who are you with when this habit happens?

  _____
  _____
  _____

- **Environmental Cues:** What environmental factors are present when this habit occurs?

  _____
  _____
  _____

Section 2: Managing Cues

- **Negative Cues:**

  List any negative cues that trigger unwanted habits.

  _____
  _____
  _____
  _____

- **Avoidance Strategy:**

  How can you avoid or minimize exposure to these cues?

  _____
  _____
  _____

- **Positive Cues:**

  List any positive cues that could help trigger desired habits.

  _____
  _____
  _____
  _____

- **Implementation Strategy:**
   How can you incorporate these positive cues into your daily routine?

   _____
   _____
   _____
   _____
   _____
   _____

For more resources, follow step-by-step:
- Scan the QR-code
- Register/Login Using Email-Id or Phone No.
- Browse through course videos
- Access Feeds for daily motivational & tricks for habit transformation

1.3.3. Sample filled-up Worksheet for a Disciplined Person:

Section 1: Identifying Cues

- **Habit:** Consistent daily schedules.
- **Time-Based Cues:** This habit typically occurs in the early morning and late afternoon, around the same times every day.
- **Location-Based Cues:** Usually, I'm at my study desk in a quiet, well-organized area of my room or at the library.
- **Emotional Cues:** I feel focused, determined, and sometimes excited about the progress I'm making.
- **Social Cues:** I'm often alone when studying, but sometimes I study with a group of like-minded peers who share similar academic goals.
- **Environmental Cues:** A clean desk, a visible study schedule, and all necessary study materials ready and organized on my desk trigger my study habits.

Section 2: Managing Cues

- **Negative Cues:** Rarely face negative cues, but sometimes, social media or unexpected interruptions can be distracting.
- **Avoidance Strategy:** I minimize distractions by keeping my phone on silent or in another room, using apps that block social media during study times, and communicating my study schedule to others to avoid interruptions.
- **Positive Cues:** A well-organized dedicated area for personal activities, a clear to-do list, and small rewards for completing study sessions serve as positive cues.
- **Implementation Strategy:** I incorporate these positive cues by starting each session with a brief review of my goals for the day, using motivational quotes or reminders, and setting a timer to track my study intervals. I also reward myself with short breaks or a treat after completing key tasks.

1.3.4. Sample filled-up Worksheet for a struggling professional:

Section 1: Identifying Cues

- **Habit:**
  Checking emails repeatedly throughout the day, often leading to distraction.

- **Time-Based Cues:** This habit tends to occur frequently mid-morning and mid-afternoon, especially when feeling less productive.

- **Location-Based Cues:** Usually happens at my desk while working on tasks that require focus.

- **Emotional Cues:** I feel anxious about missing important updates and sometimes experience boredom or stress during tedious tasks.

- **Social Cues:** I'm usually alone, but occasionally notifications from colleagues prompt me to check my inbox.

- **Environmental Cues:** Email notifications and an open inbox tab serve as visual reminders, tempting me to check for updates.

Section 2: Managing Cues

- **Negative Cues:**
    - Email notifications and an open inbox are frequent distractions, often pulling me away from focused work.
    - Boredom or stress during tasks that feel repetitive.

- **Avoidance Strategy:**
    - Turn off email notifications during focused work times and close the inbox tab to reduce the temptation to check emails.
    - Break larger tasks into smaller, engaging segments to avoid boredom.

- **Positive Cues:**
    - Using time-based reminders for dedicated email-checking sessions.

- A checklist to track task completion, keeping motivation high.

- **Implementation Strategy:**
    - Set alarms to check emails at designated times, like mid-morning and just before the day ends. Use a checklist to track and celebrate task progress, reinforcing focus on essential work.

For more resources, follow step-by-step:

- Scan the QR-code
- Register/Login Using Email-Id or Phone No.
- Browse through course videos
- Access Feeds for daily motivational & tricks for habit transformation

1.4. Mission 1 Day 4: Routines: Building the Right Actions

1.4.1. Theory

Routines are the actions we take following a cue, leading to a reward. They are the core of habits and can be shaped to create positive behaviours for lasting change. For example, brushing your teeth every night before bed is a routine triggered by the cue of feeling ready for sleep.

The Power of Routines

- **Routines are the core of habits:** They form the actions we repeat regularly, becoming second nature over time.
- **Consistent routines lead to automatic behaviours:** When performed frequently, routines transform into habits that require little conscious thought.
- **Positive routines can replace negative habits:** By focusing on creating beneficial routines, you can phase out those that don't serve you.

Building Positive Routines

- **Start small:** Begin with simple, manageable actions. If a routine is too complex, you might struggle to maintain it. For instance, starting with a 5-minute walk each morning is easier to sustain than an hour-long workout.
- **Be consistent:** Perform the routine at the same time or in response to the same cue daily. This regularity reinforces the behaviour, helping it become a habit.
- **Pair with a cue:** Use a strong cue to trigger the routine, like setting an alarm as a reminder to drink water.

Replacing Negative Routines

- **Identify the negative routine:** Recognize the action and the cue that triggers it.
- **Replace it with a positive action:** Choose a new routine that offers a similar reward. For example, replace the routine of snacking when bored with taking a short walk.
- **Reinforce the positive:** Gradually phase out the negative routine by consistently practising the positive one.

Practical Example: Building a New Routine

- **Cue:** Feeling sluggish in the afternoon.
- **New Routine:** Go for a 5-minute walk instead of drinking coffee.
- **Reward:** Feel refreshed and energized.

Why it matters?

Routines create structure, enabling you to channel your energy into purposeful actions. They transform effort into efficiency by reducing decision fatigue, freeing up mental bandwidth for growth and creativity. Building effective routines ensures consistency, a cornerstone of personal development. Over time, these routines evolve into habits, seamlessly integrating into your lifestyle. They act as a stabilizing force, especially during periods of change or uncertainty. Whether improving health, productivity, or relationships, strong routines provide the foundation for achieving long-term goals. By mastering routines, you take control of your daily actions, setting the stage for continuous improvement and success.

Inspiring Thoughts to Reflect On

Robin Sharma, a leadership expert and author, advocates for carefully structured routines as a foundation for long-term success. He quoted —

"Your daily routine is the blueprint for your success."

For more resources, follow step-by-step:

- Scan the QR-code
- Register/Login Using Email-Id or Phone No.
- Browse through course videos
- Access Feeds for daily motivational & tricks for habit transformation

1.4.2. Mission 1 Day 4 Worksheet:

Introduction: Understand how to create and maintain positive routines that lead to lasting habit changes. Focus on Identifying existing routines, replacing negative routines, and building new positive ones.

Worksheet Sections:

Section 1: Understanding Your Current Routines

1. **Identify Your Routine:**
    - List three routines you perform daily without much thought.
        - Example: Brushing your teeth, checking your phone first thing in the morning, etc.

_____

_____

_____

_____

2. **Routine Analysis:**

For each routine, identify the cue that triggers it and the reward that follows.

- Routine:

_____

- Cue:

_____

- Reward:

_____

Section 2: Replacing Negative Routines

1. **Identify a Negative Routine:**

   Describe one routine you wish to change. What is the cue that triggers it?

   - Negative Routine:

   _____

   - Cue:

   _____

2. **Develop a Positive Replacement:**

   What positive routine can you replace it with that leads to a similar reward?

   - New Routine:

   _____

   - Expected Reward:

   _____

3. **Action Plan:**

   Steps to implement the new routine:

   - Step 1:

   _____

   - Step 2:

   _____

   - Step 3:

   _____

Section 3: Building New Positive Routines

1. **Choose a Routine to Build:**

Select one new habit you want to develop (e.g., exercising daily).

New Routine:

_____

2. **Pairing with a Cue:**

Identify a strong cue that will remind you to perform this routine.

Cue:

_____

_____

3. **Designing the Routine:**

Outline the steps for your new routine:

- Step 1:

_____

- Step 2:

_____

- Step 3:

_____

4. **Reward System:**

Define a reward that will reinforce the new routine:

- Reward:

_____

_____

Section 4: Reflection and Adjustment

1. **Evaluate Your Routine:**

   After one Mission, reflect on your progress with the new routine.

   - What worked well?

   _____
   _____
   _____
   _____

   - What challenges did you face?

   _____
   _____
   _____
   _____

2. **Adjustments Needed:**

   List any changes you will make to improve your routine.

   - Adjustments:

   _____
   _____
   _____
   _____

Section 5: Action Plan for Consistency

1. **Set a Consistency Goal:**

Decide how often you will perform the new routine.

- Frequency (e.g., daily, three times a Mission):

_____

2. **Tracking Progress:**

Choose a method to track your routine (e.g., habit tracker app, journal).

- Tracking Method:

_____

_____

_____

3. **Accountability Partner:**

Who can help keep you accountable for maintaining your routine?

- Accountability Partner:

_____

_____

_____

For more resources, follow step-by-step:

- Scan the QR-code
- Register/Login Using Email-Id or Phone No.
- Browse through course videos
- Access Feeds for daily motivational & tricks for habit transformation

1.4.3. Sample filled-up Worksheet for a disciplined retired person:

Section 1: Understanding Your Current Routines

1. **Identify Your Routine:**
   - **Routine 1:** Making coffee first thing in the morning.
   - **Routine 2:** Reading the newspaper after breakfast.
   - **Routine 3:** Taking a walk around the neighborhood in the late afternoon.

2. **Routine Analysis:**
   - **Routine 1:**
     - **Cue:** Waking up.
     - **Reward:** Feeling alert and prepared for the day.
   - **Routine 2:**
     - **Cue:** Finishing breakfast.
     - **Reward:** Staying informed and starting the day with a sense of calm.
   - **Routine 3:**
     - **Cue:** The late afternoon, often around 4 PM.
     - **Reward:** Physical exercise and fresh air.

Section 2: Replacing Negative Routines

1. **Identify a Negative Routine:**
   - **Negative Routine:** Watching TV for several hours before bedtime.
   - **Cue:** Feeling tired or bored in the evening.

2. **Develop a Positive Replacement:**

- **New Routine:** Reading a book or practicing gentle stretching before bed.
- **Expected Reward:** Relaxation without the screen's stimulation, leading to better sleep quality.

3. **Action Plan:**
   - **Step 1:** Place a book or stretching mat in the living room to encourage the new habit.
   - **Step 2:** Set a reminder to start winding down with a book or stretches around 8 PM.
   - **Step 3:** Turn off the TV by 8 PM to signal the start of the new routine.

Section 3: Building New Positive Routines

1. **Choose a Routine to Build:**
   - **New Routine:** Exercising daily, such as a morning stretching routine.

2. **Pairing with a Cue:**
   - **Cue:** After making coffee in the morning.

3. **Designing the Routine:**
   - **Step 1:** Place a yoga mat in the living room.
   - **Step 2:** Do 5–10 minutes of stretching while waiting for coffee to brew.
   - **Step 3:** Finish with deep breathing exercises to set a calm, focused tone for the day.

4. **Reward System:**
   - **Reward:** A sense of accomplishment and relaxation, plus the enjoyment of a fresh cup of coffee right after.

Section 4: Reflection and Adjustment

1. **Evaluate Your Routine:**
   - **What worked well?** The morning coffee cue was a strong reminder, and the stretching added a refreshing start to the day.
   - **What challenges did you face?** Sometimes feeling rushed, which led to skipping the stretching routine.
2. **Adjustments Needed:**
   - **Adjustments:** Set coffee to brew automatically five minutes earlier to allow time for stretching.

Section 5: Action Plan for Consistency

1. **Set a Consistency Goal:**
   - **Frequency:** Daily.
2. **Tracking Progress:**
   - **Tracking Method:** Use a habit tracker app to mark off each day's stretching.
3. **Accountability Partner:**
   - **Accountability Partner:** A friend who also wants to build a morning exercise routine. We'll check in weekly to share our progress.

1.4.4. Sample filled-up Worksheet for a Struggling Person:

Section 1: Understanding Your Current Routines

1. **Identify Your Routine:**
   - List three routines you perform daily without much thought.
     - **Routine 1**: Checking social media first thing in the morning.

- **Routine 2**: Skipping breakfast and grabbing a snack later.
- **Routine 3**: Procrastinating on homework by watching videos.

2. **Routine Analysis:**
    - For each routine, identify the cue that triggers it and the reward that follows.
        - Routine: Checking social media.
            - **Cue**: Waking up and reaching for the phone.
            - **Reward**: Quick entertainment and distraction.
        - Routine: Skipping breakfast.
            - **Cue**: Running late for school.
            - **Reward**: More time in the morning to prepare but leads to hunger later.
        - Routine: Procrastinating on homework.
            - **Cue**: Feeling overwhelmed by the amount of work.
            - **Reward**: Temporary relief from stress.

Section 2: Replacing Negative Routines

1. **Identify a Negative Routine:**
    - Describe one routine you wish to change. What is the cue that triggers it?
        - **Negative Routine**: Procrastinating on homework by watching videos.
        - **Cue**: Feeling overwhelmed when thinking about assignments.

2. **Develop a Positive Replacement:**
   - What positive routine can you replace it with that leads to a similar reward?
     - **New Routine:** Break down assignments into smaller, manageable tasks and start with a 5-minute focus session.
     - **Expected Reward**: A sense of accomplishment from completing a small task, leading to reduced stress.
3. **Action Plan:**
   - Steps to implement the new routine:
     - **Step 1**: List all assignments and break them down into smaller tasks.
     - **Step 2**: Set a timer for 5 minutes to start working on the first task.
     - **Step 3**: Gradually increase the time if feeling comfortable and take short breaks.

Section 3: Building New Positive Routines

1. **Choose a Routine to Build:**
   - Select one new habit you want to develop.
     - **New Routine**: Exercising for 10 minutes every morning.
2. **Pairing with a Cue:**
   - Identify a strong cue that will remind you to perform this routine.
     - **Cue**: Right after waking up and before checking the phone.
3. **Designing the Routine:**
   - Outline the steps for your new routine:

- **Step 1**: Place workout clothes next to the bed the night before.
- **Step 2**: Do 10 minutes of simple exercises like stretching and jumping jacks.
- **Step 3**: Reward yourself with a refreshing shower or listening to a favourite song.

4. **Reward System:**
   - Define a reward that will reinforce the new routine:
     - Reward: Feeling more awake and energized for the day ahead and allowing 5 minutes of social media after exercise.

Section 4: Reflection and Adjustment

1. **Evaluate Your Routine:**
   - After one Mission, reflect on your progress with the new routine.
     - **What worked well?**

     Starting small with 5-minute tasks helped reduce overwhelm.
     - **What challenges did you face?**

     Struggling to resist the urge to check the phone first.

2. **Adjustments Needed:**
   - **List any changes you will make to improve your routine.**
     - **Adjustments:** Move the phone to another room overnight to reduce temptation. Consider finding an accountability partner for morning exercises.

Section 5: Action Plan for Consistency

1. **Set a Consistency Goal:**
   - Decide how often you will perform the new routine.
     - **Frequency**: Daily exercise and study sessions after school are held every day.

2. **Tracking Progress:**
   - Choose a method to track your routine.
     - **Tracking Method**: Use a habit-tracking app to check off completed tasks and exercise sessions.

3. **Accountability Partner:**
   - Who can help keep you accountable for maintaining your routine?
     - Accountability Partner: A friend who also wants to develop good study and exercise habits.

For more resources, follow step-by-step:

- Scan the QR-code
- Register/Login Using Email-Id or Phone No.
- Browse through course videos
- Access Feeds for daily motivational & tricks for habit transformation

1.5. Mission 1 Day 5: Rewards: Reinforcing Positive Habits

1.5.1. Theory

A **reward** is the positive outcome or benefit gained from a routine. It serves as a key motivator for repeating the behaviour. Rewards are essential for making habits stick. They provide positive feedback that reinforces the habit loop, making the behaviour more likely to be repeated. Understanding how to select and use rewards effectively can significantly influence your success in habit formation.

The Role of Rewards in Habit Formation

- **Rewards reinforce the habit loop:** They provide positive feedback that makes you want to repeat the behaviour. Without a reward, the habit loop (Cue → Routine → Reward) remains incomplete.
- **Consistent rewards make habits stick:** When the reward is satisfying and immediate, it strengthens the habit, turning it into an automatic behaviour over time.
- **Anticipation of the reward:** The expectation of a reward can become a cue, motivating you to engage in the habit.

Identifying Effective Rewards

- **Immediate and Satisfying:** Choose rewards that provide instant gratification, like enjoying a relaxing shower after a workout.
- **Aligned with Goals:** The reward should support your long-term objectives. If your goal is to get fit, a healthy smoothie might be a better reward than a sugary treat.
- **Experiment:** Try different rewards to see which ones motivate you the most. Test and refine until you find what works best.

Avoiding Negative Rewards

- **Beware of rewards that undermine progress:** For example, overeating after exercising can counteract your fitness goals.
- **Choose positive rewards:** Opt for rewards that promote well-being and success, like treating yourself to a new book instead of junk food.
- **Replace harmful rewards:** Swap out negative rewards with healthier alternatives to support your habit journey.

Practical Example: Reinforcing a Habit with Rewards

- **Routine:** Exercising for 30 minutes.
- **Reward:** Watching your favourite TV show afterwardss.
- **Outcome:** The anticipation of watching the show motivates you to complete your workout.

Why it matters?

Rewards are essential for reinforcing positive habits, making them stick. They provide immediate satisfaction, which motivates you to repeat behaviors until they become second nature. Using well-aligned rewards ensures your efforts feel meaningful and enjoyable, sustaining your commitment over time. This approach balances discipline with gratification, creating a sense of accomplishment and joy in the growth process. Rewards also help you measure progress, fostering a sense of achievement that propels you forward. By mastering reinforcement, you cultivate a growth-friendly mindset, ensuring that self-improvement becomes a rewarding and self-sustaining cycle.

Inspiring Thoughts to Reflect On

B.F. Skinner, a renowned American psychologist, was a leading figure in behavioral psychology and the development of operant conditioning. His groundbreaking work in reinforcement theory demonstrated how rewards and consequences shape human and animal behavior, leaving a lasting impact on psychology, education, and behavior modification practices. He said —

> "Behavior that's rewarded is behavior that gets repeated."

1.5.2. Mission 1 Day 5 Worksheet:

Worksheet Sections:

Part 1: Understanding Your Rewards

Fill in the Blanks:

- A reward is the _____ outcome or benefit gained from a routine.
- The _____ of a reward can trigger the habit and make it more likely to be repeated.
- Effective rewards should be _____ and align with your _____.

Short Answer:

- What is an example of a reward you currently use to reinforce a positive habit? How does it motivate you to keep the habit?

Part 2: Identifying Effective Rewards

Exercise: Identifying Your Habit Rewards

- Think about a habit you want to build or strengthen. Identify potential rewards that would motivate you to perform this habit consistently. Use the table below to brainstorm:

Habit	Potential Reward
Example: Exercising daily	Watching a favourite TV show after

Multiple Choice:

Which of the following characteristics make a reward most effective? (Circle all that apply)

    a) Immediate

    b) Aligned with long-term goals

    c) Requires waiting for a month

    d) Small and satisfying

Part 3: Evaluating Your Current Rewards

Reflection Questions:

Are there any rewards you use that might undermine your progress? If so, what are they?

_____

_____

_____

What is one positive reward you can use to replace a negative one?

_____

_____

_____

Fill in the Blanks:

To avoid negative rewards, choose rewards that _____ your well-being and long-term _____.

Part 4: Creating a Reward Plan

Exercise: Design a Reward System

- Choose a new habit you want to develop. Complete the reward plan below to help reinforce this habit.

New Habit	Cue	Routine	Reward

- How will the reward you chose for this new habit help reinforce the behaviour?

_____

_____

_____

_____

For more resources, follow step-by-step:

- Scan the QR-code
- Register/Login Using Email-Id or Phone No.
- Browse through course videos
- Access Feeds for daily motivational & tricks for habit transformation

1.5.3. Sample filled-up Worksheet for a Disciplined Person:

Part 1: Understanding Your Rewards

1. **Fill in the Blanks:**
   - A reward is the **positive** outcome or benefit gained from a routine.
   - The **anticipation** of a reward can trigger the habit and make it more likely to be repeated.
   - Effective rewards should be **immediate** and align with your **goals**.

2. **Short Answer:**
   - What is an example of a reward you currently use to reinforce a positive habit? How does it motivate you to keep the habit?
     - **Example:** After completing my morning workout, I reward myself with a fresh fruit smoothie. This motivates me because I love smoothies, and they also align with my goal of maintaining a healthy lifestyle.

Part 2: Identifying Effective Rewards

3. **Exercise: Identifying Your Habit Rewards**
   - Think about a habit you want to build or strengthen. Identify potential rewards that would motivate you to perform this habit consistently. Use the table below to brainstorm:

Habit	Potential Reward
Exercising daily	Watching a favourite TV show after
Reading for 20 minutes	Enjoying a piece of dark chocolate
Meditating each evening	Taking a relaxing bath

4. **Multiple Choice:**
   - Which of the following characteristics make a reward most effective? (Circle all that apply)
     - a) Immediate
     - b) Aligned with long-term goals
     - **d) Small and satisfying**

Part 3: Evaluating Your Current Rewards

5. **Reflections: Are there any rewards you use that might undermine your progress? If so, what are they?**

   Yes, sometimes I reward myself with a high-calorie dessert after a workout. This undermines my fitness progress.

   What is one positive reward you can use to replace a negative one?

   I can replace the dessert with a fruit salad or a refreshing glass of lemon water.

6. **Fill in the Blanks:**
   - To avoid negative rewards, choose rewards that **promote** your well-being and long-term **success**.

Part 4: Creating a Reward Plan

7. **Exercise: Design a Reward System**

Choose a new habit you want to develop. Complete the reward plan below to help reinforce this habit.

New Habit	Cue	Routine	Reward
Studying for an hour	7:00 PM daily	Study for 1 hour	Enjoy a cup of herbal tea

8. How will the reward you chose for this new habit help reinforce the behaviour?

Drinking herbal tea is a soothing and enjoyable experience for me. Having this reward to look forward to makes studying feel less like a chore and more like a part of a relaxing evening routine.

1.5.4. Sample filled-up Worksheet for a Struggling Person:

Part 1: Understanding Your Rewards

Fill in the Blanks:

- A reward is the **positive** outcome or benefit gained from a routine.
- The **anticipation** of a reward can trigger the habit and make it more likely to be repeated.
- Effective rewards should be **immediate** and align with your **goals**.

Short Answer:

- **What is an example of a reward you currently use to reinforce a positive habit? How does it motivate you to keep the habit?** An example is taking a short break after completing a challenging task. This helps me recharge and encourages me to stay productive and focused.

Part 2: Identifying Effective Rewards

Exercise: Identifying Your Habit Rewards

- Think about a habit you want to build or strengthen. Identify potential rewards that would motivate you to perform this habit consistently.

Habit	Potential Reward
Managing emails daily	Treating myself to a coffee break
Preparing for meetings	Listening to a favorite podcast afterward
Finishing daily reports	Taking a 10-minute walk outside

Multiple Choice:

Which of the following characteristics make a reward most effective? (Circle all that apply)

- a) Immediate
- b) Aligned with long-term goals
- c) Small and satisfying

Part 3: Evaluating Your Current Rewards

Reflection Questions:

- **Are there any rewards you use that might undermine your progress? If so, what are they?**

    Yes, scrolling through social media after completing a task sometimes takes longer than expected and disrupts my productivity.

- **What is one positive reward you can use to replace a negative one?**
    Replacing social media scrolling with a quick stretch or a short walk can refresh my mind without taking up too much time.

Fill in the Blanks:

To avoid negative rewards, choose rewards that **support** your well-being and long-term **goals**.

Part 4: Creating a Reward Plan

Exercise: Design a Reward System

- Choose a new habit you want to develop. Complete the reward plan below to help reinforce this habit.

New Habit	Cue	Routine	Reward
Organizing desk daily	End of workday	Clear desk, arrange items	10 minutes of relaxation time

- **How will the reward you chose for this new habit help reinforce the behavior?**

Relaxation time provides a sense of closure to the workday and makes the habit of organizing my desk more enjoyable and rewarding.

For more resources, follow step-by-step:

- Scan the QR-code
- Register/Login Using Email-Id or Phone No.
- Browse through course videos
- Access Feeds for daily motivational & tricks for habit transformation

1.6. Mission 1 Day 6: Habit Tracking: Monitoring Progress

1.6.1. Theory

Habit tracking is the practice of recording your progress in building or changing habits. It provides a clear visual representation of your efforts, helping you stay motivated and accountable.

Example: Marking off each day on a calendar when you complete a habit, like exercising, is a straightforward way to visualize your progress.

The Benefits of Habit Tracking

- **Increases accountability and commitment:** When you track your habits, you hold yourself accountable, which strengthens your commitment to follow through.
- **Provides visual motivation:** Seeing progress, like a streak of completed days, gives you a sense of accomplishment and motivates you to keep going.
- **Helps identify patterns:** Tracking allows you to notice trends and obstacles, such as specific days or circumstances where you struggle to maintain the habit. This awareness is key to making adjustments.

How to Track Your Habits

- **Use a habit tracker:** Whether it's a calendar, a smartphone app, or a journal, find a tracking method that suits you.
- **Track one habit at a time:** Focusing on one habit reduces overwhelm and increases the chances of success.
- **Record progress consistently:** Set a routine to log your progress daily or monthly to maintain consistency and build momentum.

Analyzing Your Habit Data

- **Look for trends:** Review your habit-tracking data to identify days missed and patterns of success.
- **Identify obstacles:** Pinpoint triggers or obstacles that hinder your progress, allowing you to address them proactively.
- **Adjust your approach:** Use the insights from your tracking data to tweak your routine and optimize your chances of success.

Why it matters?

Habit monitoring is a powerful tool for turning intentions into actions. It increases accountability, provides a visual reminder of your efforts, and highlights patterns in your behavior. By consistently monitoring progress, you gain insights into what works and what doesn't, enabling you to make adjustments for sustained growth. Tracking builds momentum by rewarding consistency and reinforcing a sense of accomplishment. It transforms habit-building from a vague concept into a tangible process, helping you stay motivated and committed to your personal development journey.

Inspiring Thoughts to Reflect On

The best way to predict your future is to create it—and tracking helps you do just that. As Marie Forleo, a successful entrepreneur, author, and motivational speaker said —

"Success doesn't come from what you do occasionally, but what you do consistently."

For more resources, follow step-by-step:

- Scan the QR-code
- Register/Login Using Email-Id or Phone No.
- Browse through course videos
- Access Feeds for daily motivational & tricks for habit transformation

1.6.2. Mission 1 Day 6 Worksheet:

Worksheet Sections:

Part 1: Understanding Rewards

1. **Fill in the Blanks:**
    - A reward is the _____ outcome or benefit gained from a routine.
    - Consistent rewards help to _____ the habit loop.
    - Effective rewards should be _____ and _____ with your goals.

2. **Multiple Choice:**
    - What is the most effective type of reward for reinforcing a habit?
        - a) Something that aligns with your long-term goals.
        - b) Something that is easy to obtain, regardless of its impact.
        - c) A reward that involves a negative behaviour, like eating junk food.
    - **Why did you choose your answer?**

    _____

    _____

    _____

Part 2: Identifying Your Rewards

3. **Short Answer:**
    - Think of a positive habit you are trying to build.
    - What reward do you currently use (or could you use) to motivate yourself to stick with it?

_____

_____

_____

_____

_____

4. **Exercise: List Your Reward Options**

Choose a habit you want to strengthen. Identify 3 possible rewards that could motivate you to maintain this habit. Then, select the reward that best aligns with your goals.

Habit	Possible Rewards	Chosen Reward
Example: Exercising	Watching a TV show, taking a warm bath, a smoothie	Taking a warm bath

Part 3: Evaluating Your Current Rewards

5. **Fill in the Blanks:**
   - Avoid rewards that _____ your progress. Instead, choose rewards that promote _____ and align with your values.

6. **Reflection Questions:**
   - Do any of the rewards you use currently undermine your progress? If so, what are they, and how can you replace them with positive alternatives?

   _____

   _____

   _____

   - How do you feel after using your chosen reward? Does it make you more likely to repeat the habit?

   _____

   _____

   _____

   _____

Part 4: Planning Your Reward System

7. **Exercise: Create a Reward Plan**
   - Select a habit you want to build. Identify a cue, routine, and reward to help reinforce this habit.

Habit	Cue	Routine	Reward
Example: Reading nightly	Seeing a book on the nightstand	Read for 15 minutes	Enjoy a cup of herbal tea

8. **Short Answer:**

How will the reward you chose help reinforce the behaviour? Explain why you think this reward will be effective.

_____

_____

_____

_____

For more resources, follow step-by-step:

- Scan the QR-code
- Register/Login Using Email-Id or Phone No.
- Browse through course videos
- Access Feeds for daily motivational & tricks for habit transformation

1.6.3. Sample filled-up Worksheet for a Disciplined Person:

Part 1: Understanding Rewards

1. Fill in the Blanks:

- A reward is the **positive** outcome or benefit gained from a routine.
- Consistent rewards help to **strengthen** the habit loop.
- Effective rewards should be **immediate** and **aligned** with your goals.

2. Multiple Choice:

- **What is the most effective type of reward for reinforcing a habit?**
  - **a)** Something that aligns with your long-term goals.
- **Why did you choose your answer?**

  Because rewards that support long-term goals reinforce positive behavior in ways that align with desired outcomes, making it easier to continue the habit without negative impacts.

Part 2: Identifying Your Rewards

3. Short Answer:

- **Think of a positive habit you are trying to build.** Organizing my workspace daily.
- **What reward do you currently use (or could you use) to motivate yourself to stick with it?**

  After organizing, I take a short break to relax with a cup of coffee, which helps me enjoy a clear workspace and recharges me for the next tasks.

4. Exercise: List Your Reward Options

- Choose a habit you want to strengthen. Identify 3 possible rewards that could motivate you to maintain this habit. Then, select the reward that best aligns with your goals.

Habit	Possible Rewards	Chosen Reward
Checking emails	Take a short walk, 5 minutes of stretching, listen to a favorite song	Take a short walk
Preparing for meetings	Read a motivational quote, enjoy a healthy snack, take a 5-minute break	Take a 5-minute break
Completing daily reports	Check off task list, journal accomplishments, listen to relaxing music	Journal accomplishments

Part 3: Evaluating Your Current Rewards

5. Fill in the Blanks:

- Avoid rewards that **disrupt** your progress. Instead, choose rewards that promote **growth** and align with your values.

6. Reflection Questions:

- **Do any of the rewards you use currently undermine your progress? If so, what are they, and how can you replace them with positive alternatives?**

    Occasionally, I reward myself with screen time, like browsing on my phone, which can sometimes distract me longer than planned. I could replace this with a short walk or quick stretching exercise.

- **How do you feel after using your chosen reward? Does it make you more likely to repeat the habit?**

    Yes, taking a short break after a focused work session refreshes me, making it easier to start the next task with a clear mind. It helps reinforce my productivity routine.

Part 4: Planning Your Reward System

7. Exercise: Create a Reward Plan

- Select a habit you want to build. Identify a cue, routine, and reward to help reinforce this habit.

Habit	Cue	Routine	Reward
Reading daily	Seeing a book on the desk	Read for 15 minutes	Enjoy a cup of herbal tea
Organizing workspace	End of workday	Tidy up desk	Relax with a coffee
Stretching regularly	10 a.m. alert	5 minutes of stretching	Listen to a favorite song

8. **Short Answer:**

- **How will the reward you chose help reinforce the behavior? Explain why you think this reward will be effective.** Each reward is simple, satisfying, and quick, making it easy to stick to the routine without losing momentum. For instance, taking a short coffee break after tidying my workspace makes organizing feel refreshing and positive, increasing the likelihood that I'll repeat it daily.

1.6.4. Sample filled-up Worksheet for a Struggling Person:

Part 1: Understanding Rewards

1. **Fill in the Blanks:**
    - A reward is the **positive** outcome or benefit gained from a routine.
    - Consistent rewards help to **reinforce** the habit loop.
    - Effective rewards should be **immediate** and **aligned** with your goals.

2. **Multiple Choice:**
    - **What is the most effective type of reward for reinforcing a habit?**

    a) **Something that aligns with your long-term goals.**

- Why did you choose your answer?

    I chose this because I understand that long-term rewards are supposed to help, but honestly, I struggle to choose rewards that actually motivate me right now.

Part 2: Identifying Your Rewards

3. Think of a positive habit you are trying to build. What reward do you currently use (or could you use) to motivate yourself to stick with it?

    - I've been trying to build a habit of exercising, but I often skip it. I sometimes tell myself I can have a treat afterwardss, but that doesn't always feel like the best choice.

4. **Exercise: List Your Reward Options**

    - Choose a habit you want to strengthen. Identify 3 possible rewards that could motivate you to maintain this habit. Then, select the reward that best aligns with your goals.

Habit	Possible Rewards	Chosen Reward
Exercising	Eating a snack, watching TV, scrolling social media	Watching TV
Reading before bed	Playing a game, scrolling social media, having tea	Scrolling social media
Drinking more water	Eating a cookie, taking a break, checking my phone	Checking my phone

Part 3: Evaluating Your Current Rewards

5. **Fill in the Blanks:**
    - Avoid rewards that **undermine** your progress. Instead, choose rewards that promote **well-being** and align with your values.

6. **Reflections:**
    - **Do any of the rewards you use currently undermine your progress? If so, what are they, and how can you replace them with positive alternatives?**
        - Yes, I tend to reward myself with snacks or screen time, but they don't really help me stay on track. I could try replacing them with something healthier, but I'm not sure what else would motivate me.
    - **How do you feel after using your chosen reward? Does it make you more likely to repeat the habit?**
        - Honestly, no. I feel like I just go back to old habits, and the reward doesn't really help me stick with the positive changes.

Part 4: Planning Your Reward System

7. **Exercise: Create a Reward Plan**
    - Select a habit you want to build. Identify a cue, routine, and reward to help reinforce this habit.

Habit	Cue	Routine	Reward
Reading nightly	Feeling tired at night	Read for 10 minutes	Scroll social media
Exercising	Feeling sluggish in the afternoon	Do 10 minutes of exercise	Watch a show
Drinking more water	Feeling thirsty	Drink a glass of water	Check my phone

8. **How will the reward you chose help reinforce the behaviour? Explain why you think this reward will be effective.**

    I'm not sure if these rewards will work. I feel like I always end up doing the same thing anyway, like watching TV or scrolling social media, and it doesn't really motivate me to keep up with the habits.

1.7. Mission 1 Day 7: Reviewing and Adjusting Your Habits

1.7.1. Theory

Reviewing and adjusting your habits is a vital part of creating long-term, positive change. While building habits requires consistency and effort, regular reflection ensures that your routines align with your goals and adapt to changes in your life. Habit reviews help identify what's working and what's not, allowing you to make improvements for ongoing success.

The Importance of Reviewing Your Habits

- Regular habit reviews provide insight into your progress and help you identify the strengths and weaknesses of your routines. By analyzing your efforts, you can spot trends, notice patterns, and address obstacles that might be hindering your success. Continuous improvement is the foundation of effective habit-building; without it, you risk getting stuck in unproductive routines.
- **Example:** Imagine you've been trying to wake up early but keep hitting the snooze button. By reviewing this habit, you may realize that going to bed too late is the issue. Recognizing this allows you to adjust your bedtime to support your goal of waking up early.

How to Review Your Habits

- **Set a Regular Review Schedule:** Make it a habit to review your progress on a Mission or monthly basis. Scheduling regular check-ins ensures you stay mindful of your habits and can make timely adjustments.
- **Analyze Your Habit Tracking Data:** Use your tracking data to identify patterns and trends. Are there specific days you're more successful? Are there consistent obstacles?
- **Reflect on Successes and Challenges:** Take time to consider what worked well and what didn't. Understanding both successes and challenges helps you fine-tune your approach.

Adjusting Your Habits

- Small, incremental changes are often the most effective way to adjust habits. If a routine isn't yielding the desired results, try modifying one aspect at a time, such as adjusting your cue, routine, or reward.

- Experiment with different approaches until you find what works best for you. Being flexible and willing to adapt your habits as your circumstances change is crucial for long-term success.

Why it matters?

Reviewing and adjusting your habits matters because it helps create lasting, positive change by aligning your routines with your evolving goals. Consistency in habit-building is essential, yet reflection offers the chance to fine-tune what isn't working, enhancing effectiveness. Without regular review, it's easy to fall into unproductive routines that don't support your aspirations. Adjustments based on tracking data and self-reflection can overcome obstacles and optimize your progress, supporting long-term success.

Inspiring Thoughts to Reflect On

"Success is the sum of small efforts, repeated day in and day out," said Robert Collier, an influential American author of the early 20th century renowned for his works on self-improvement and personal success. His writings urged readers to embrace the power of consistent effort and incremental progress. Similarly, Lao Tzu, the ancient Chinese philosopher widely regarded as the father of Taoism, taught that "the journey of a thousand miles begins with one step." His teachings emphasize harmony and purposeful action, underscoring that great achievements start with small, deliberate steps—reinforcing the transformative power of steady, continuous effort.

For more resources, follow step-by-step:

- Scan the QR-code
- Register/Login Using Email-Id or Phone No.
- Browse through course videos
- Access Feeds for daily motivational & tricks for habit transformation

1.7.2. Mission 1 Day 7 Worksheet:

Worksheet Sections:

Part 1: The Importance of Reviewing Habits
1. **Fill in the Blanks:**
    - Regular habit reviews help identify what's _____ and what's _____.
    - Continuous _____ is key to long-term habit success.
2. **Short Answer:**
    - Why do you think it's important to regularly review your habits?

    _____

    _____

    _____

Part 2: Reviewing Your Current Habits
3. **Exercise: Habit Review Table**
    - Choose one habit you've been working on. Fill in the table below to reflect on your progress.

Habit	Successes	Challenges	Tracking Data

4. **Reflection Questions:**

What patterns or trends have you noticed from tracking this habit?

_____

_____

_____

Are there specific situations or times when you struggle with this habit?

_____

_____

_____

Part 3: Adjusting Your Habits

5. **Fill in the Blanks:**

- Make small, _____ changes to your routine if needed.

- Be _____ and willing to adapt as your circumstances change.

- Experiment _____ until you find what works best for you.

6. **Exercise: Planning Habit Adjustments**

    Based on your review, identify one adjustment you can make to your habit to improve its success.

Habit	Current Routine	Adjustment

7. **Short Answer:**

   How do you think this adjustment will help you stay on track with your habit?

   _____

   _____

   _____

Part 4: Practical Application

8. **Exercise: Create an Adjustment Plan**

   Select another habit that needs adjusting. Complete the table below with specific changes you will make.

Habit	Issue Identified	Adjustment Plan

Habit	Issue Identified	Adjustment Plan

9. **Fill in the Blanks:**

- Small _____ can lead to big changes in habit success.

- Daily milestones should be _____.

- Target milestones should be set depending upon _____ and _____.

- Try to find _____ that is stopping you from following your routine.

1.7.3. Sample filled-up Worksheet for a Disciplined Person:

Part 1: The Importance of Reviewing Habits
1. **Fill in the Blanks:**
   - Regular habit reviews help identify what's **working** and what's **not**.
   - Continuous **improvement** is key to long-term habit success.
2. **Short Answer:**
   - Why do you think it's important to regularly review your habits?
     - Regularly reviewing habits is crucial because it allows me to see what is effective and where I need to make changes. It keeps me accountable and helps me stay on track with my goals.

Part 2: Reviewing Your Current Habits
3. **Exercise: Habit Review Table**
   - Choose one habit you've been working on. Fill in the table below to reflect on your progress.

Habit	Successes	Challenges	Tracking Data
Exercising daily	Increased energy and strength	Feeling tired on busy days	Completed 5 days a Mission for 3 Missions

4. **Reflection Questions:**
   - What patterns or trends have you noticed from tracking this habit?
     - I noticed that I am more consistent with exercising on mission days when I have a set schedule. I tend

to skip workouts on mission ends, especially when I sleep in.
- o Are there specific situations or times when you struggle with this habit?
    - Yes, I struggle to exercise on mission ends and days when my schedule is more unpredictable.

Part 3: Adjusting Your Habits
5. **Fill in the Blanks:**
    - o Make small, **incremental** changes to your routine if needed.
    - o Be **flexible** and willing to adapt as your circumstances change.

6. **Exercise: Planning Habit Adjustments**
    - o Based on your review, identify one adjustment you can make to your habit to improve its success.

Habit	Current Routine	Adjustment
Exercising daily	Exercise in the evenings	Shift to morning workouts to avoid interruptions later in the day

7. **Short Answer:**
    - o How do you think this adjustment will help you stay on track with your habit?
        - Exercising in the morning will help me start the day positively and reduce the chances of missing a workout due to unexpected events or feeling tired in the evening.

Part 4: Practical Application

8. **Exercise: Create an Adjustment Plan**
   - Select another habit that needs adjusting. Complete the table below with specific changes you will make.

Habit	Issue Identified	Adjustment Plan
Reading nightly	Falling asleep before reading	Set a 10-minute timer to read earlier in the evening before bed

9. **Fill in the Blanks:**
   - Small **adjustments** can lead to big changes in habit success.
   - Daily milestones should be **small and attainable**.
   - Target milestones should be set depending upon **capabilities and priorities**.
   - Try to find the **obstacle** that is stopping you from following your routine.

1.7.4. Sample filled-up Worksheet for a Struggling Person:

Part 1: The Importance of Reviewing Habits

1. **Fill in the Blanks:**
   - Regular habit reviews help identify what's **working** and what's **not**.
   - Continuous **improvement** is key to long-term habit success.

2. **Short Answer:**
   - Why do you think it's important to regularly review your habits?

   I think it's important because sometimes my habits don't go as planned. I need to see why things aren't working, but I often feel stuck or unsure about what to change.

Part 2: Reviewing Your Current Habits

3. **Exercise: Habit Review Table**
    - Choose one habit you've been working on. Fill in the table below to reflect on your progress.

Habit	Successes	Challenges	Tracking Data
Drinking more water	Better on some days	Forgetting to drink during busy times	3-4 days a mission, inconsistent

4. **Reflection Questions:**

- What patterns or trends have you noticed from tracking this habit?

    I noticed I tend to forget to drink water when I'm busy or stressed. I also find it hard to keep track when the mission ends.

- Are there specific situations or times when you struggle with this habit?

    Yes, mostly when I'm at work or running errands. I get caught up in other things and forget to drink water.

Part 3: Adjusting Your Habits

5. **Fill in the Blanks:**
    - Make small, **incremental** changes to your routine if needed.
    - Be **flexible** and willing to adapt as your circumstances change.

6. **Exercise: Planning Habit Adjustments**
    - Based on your review, identify one adjustment you can make to your habit to improve its success.

Habit	Current Routine	Adjustment
Drinking more water	Drinking when I remember	Set a phone reminder every 2 hours to drink water

7. **Short Answer:**
    - How do you think this adjustment will help you stay on track with your habit?
        - I'm not sure if it will work, but I hope the reminders will make me more aware. I just tend to ignore reminders if I'm busy, so I'll have to see if this helps.

Part 4: Practical Application

8. **Exercise: Create an Adjustment Plan**
    - Select another habit that needs adjusting. Complete the table below with specific changes you will make.

Habit	Issue Identified	Adjustment Plan
Reading nightly	Too tired to read at night	Try reading for 5 minutes earlier in the evening, right after dinner

9. **Fill in the Blanks:**
    - Small **adjustments** can lead to big changes in habit success.
    - Daily milestones should be **small and attainable**.
    - Target milestones should be set depending upon **capabilities and priorities**.
    - Try to find the **reason** that is stopping you from following your routine.

Chapter – 2

2.1. Mission 2 Day 1: Overcoming Obstacles

2.1.1. Theory:

Forming new habits can be challenging, especially when obstacles arise that hinder progress. Understanding and overcoming these obstacles is key to building lasting, positive habits. This session focuses on identifying common challenges and strategies to conquer them, ensuring a smoother habit-building journey.

Common Obstacles to Habit Formation

- **Lack of Motivation:** It's easy to start a new habit with enthusiasm, but when that initial motivation fades, it can be hard to maintain consistency.
- **Unrealistic Goals:** Setting goals that are too ambitious or vague can lead to frustration and burnout. Clear, manageable goals are crucial for success.
- **External Distractions:** Interruptions like phone notifications, social media, or unexpected events can break your focus and disrupt habit formation.
- **Internal Resistance:** Mental barriers, such as self-doubt or fear of change, can prevent you from adopting new behaviours.

Identifying Your Personal Obstacles: To overcome obstacles, start by identifying what has hindered your progress in the past:

- Reflect on Past Failed Habits
- Consider Current Challenges:
- Seek Feedback

Strategies to Overcome Obstacles

- **Break Down Goals:** Start with small, manageable steps to prevent overwhelming situations. Instead of aiming for an hour of exercise daily, start with 10 minutes.

- **Increase Accountability:** Share your goals with a friend or join a group for support. Knowing someone is checking in on your progress can boost your commitment.
- **Minimize Distractions:** Create an environment that supports your habit. Turn off notifications, set up a dedicated workspace, or remove tempting distractions.
- **Build Resilience:** Recognize that setbacks are part of the journey. Practice patience and persistence, knowing that each step brings you closer to your goal.

Why it matters?

Obstacles are inevitable when forming new habits, but how you respond to them determines your success. By understanding the challenges that hinder progress—such as distractions, self-doubt, or lack of time—you equip yourself with the tools to overcome them. Conquering obstacles builds resilience and confidence, essential traits for sustained growth. Each hurdle you overcome strengthens your ability to tackle future challenges, transforming setbacks into opportunities for growth. This step is critical for creating a solid foundation for habit formation and personal development.

Inspiring Thoughts to Reflect On

Obstacles don't block the path. They are the path. Therefore, Joshua J. Marine quoted once,

"Challenges are what make life interesting. Overcoming them is what makes life meaningful."

Marine is an author and motivational speaker who focuses on personal development and resilience. His work highlights the importance of facing adversity and finding purpose through overcoming obstacles.

2.1.2. Mission 2 Day 1 Worksheet:

Instruction: Use this worksheet to identify the internal and external obstacles that hold you back from forming habits. Then, create a strategic action plan with concrete steps to overcome these barriers.

Worksheet Sections:

Part 1: Identifying Your Obstacles
1. What are the main internal and external obstacles you face?

_____

_____

_____

2. How have these barriers impacted your habit consistency so far?

_____

_____

_____

Part 2: Strategies for Overcoming Obstacles
1. What mindset shifts can you make to tackle internal barriers?

_____

_____

_____

2. What environmental or time-management changes can you implement?

_____

_____

_____

3. How will you stay flexible when unexpected challenges arise?

_____

_____

_____

Part 3: Creating an Action Plan

1. List the three biggest obstacles to your habit formation.

    1. _____

    2. _____

    3. _____

2. Write down one specific action you can take to overcome each obstacle.

_____

_____

_____

3. How will you track your progress and hold yourself accountable?

_____

_____

_____

2.1.3. Sample filled-up Worksheet for a Disciplined Person:

Part 1: Identifying Your Obstacles

1. **What are the main internal and external obstacles you face?**
   - **Internal:** Self-doubt and procrastination, especially when the habit seems difficult or time-consuming.
   - **External:** Busy schedule, frequent interruptions, and phone notifications that break my focus.

2. **How have these barriers impacted your habit consistency so far?**
   - These obstacles have made it difficult to establish a consistent routine. I often start strong but quickly lose momentum, especially when unexpected tasks or distractions come up. Procrastination causes me to delay starting my habits, and interruptions make it hard to maintain focus.

Part 2: Strategies for Overcoming Obstacles

1. **What mindset shifts can you make to tackle internal barriers?**
   - I will adopt a "progress over perfection" mindset to reduce self-doubt. I'll remind myself that small steps count and that consistency is more important than getting it perfect every time.

2. **What environmental or time-management changes can you implement?**
   - I will set up a dedicated, clutter-free workspace to minimize distractions. I will also schedule specific times for my habits, such as blocking out 10 minutes each morning for exercise and turning off phone notifications during these periods.

3. **How will you stay flexible when unexpected challenges arise?**
   - I'll create backup plans for busy days, like a 5-minute version of my habits if I'm short on time. I'll also practice self-compassion, acknowledging that some days will be more challenging and that it's okay to adjust my routine as needed.

Part 3: Creating an Action Plan

1. **List the three biggest obstacles to your habit formation.**
   - Procrastination
   - Distractions from phone notifications
   - Busy and unpredictable schedule

2. **Write down one specific action you can take to overcome each obstacle.**
   - **Procrastination:** Break down tasks into small, manageable steps and start with just 5 minutes.
   - **Distractions from phone notifications:** Use "Do Not Disturb" mode during habit-building times.
   - **Busy and unpredictable schedule:** Create a flexible habit plan with shorter, adaptable versions for hectic days.

3. **How will you track your progress and hold yourself accountable?**
   - I will use a habit tracker app to mark and review daily progress every Sunday evening. I'll also share my goals with a friend for added accountability and regular check-ins.

2.1.4. Sample filled-up Worksheet for a Struggling Person:

Part 1: Identifying Your Obstacles

1. **What are the main internal and external obstacles you face?**
   - **Internal:** Self-doubt, lack of motivation, and a tendency to overthink before starting.
   - **External:** Constant distractions from phone notifications, work stress, and irregular daily schedules.

2. **How have these barriers impacted your habit consistency so far?**
   - These obstacles make it hard to start or stick with any habit. I get overwhelmed easily, and when my schedule changes or I feel stressed, I often abandon the habit altogether. I also

tend to get distracted, which makes it challenging to build any routine.

Part 2: Strategies for Overcoming Obstacles
1. **What mindset shifts can you make to tackle internal barriers?**
   - I need to stop expecting myself to be perfect and accept that starting small is okay. I should try to focus on making even a little progress instead of feeling like I have to do everything at once.
2. **What environmental or time-management changes can you implement?**
   - I can try to keep my phone in another room during the time I want to work on my habits. I could also set a reminder on my phone, but I'm worried that I might just ignore it.
3. **How will you stay flexible when unexpected challenges arise?**
   - I usually struggle with this, but maybe I can make a list of "quick versions" of my habits, like 2-minute exercises or reading one page. If something comes up, at least I can do a shorter version.

Part 3: Creating an Action Plan
1. **List the three biggest obstacles to your habit formation.**
   - Procrastination due to overthinking
   - Distractions from phone notifications
   - Irregular schedule making it hard to keep routines
2. **Write down one specific action you can take to overcome each obstacle.**
   - **Procrastination:** Start with just 2 minutes of the habit, so it feels less overwhelming.
   - **Distractions from phone notifications:** Try putting my phone on "Do Not Disturb" mode, though I might still check it out of habit.

- **Irregular schedule:** Set a reminder for a small habit, but be okay with doing it at different times each day if needed.

3. **How will you track your progress and hold yourself accountable?**
   - I'll try to use a simple habit tracker, but I often forget to update it. Maybe I'll ask a friend to check in with me once a mission to see how I'm doing.

For more resources, follow step-by-step:
- Scan the QR-code
- Register/Login Using Email-Id or Phone No.
- Browse through course videos
- Access Feeds for daily motivational & tricks for habit transformation

2.2. Mission 2 Day 2: Staying Motivated

2.2.1. Theory:

Motivation is the driving force that initiates and sustains habit formation. While it provides the spark needed to start a new habit, maintaining motivation over time can be challenging. Understanding how to keep your motivation levels high is essential to building and sustaining long-term habits.

The Role of Motivation in Habit Formation

- Motivation is crucial in sparking the initial action required to form a new habit. It fuels the desire to make changes and take the first steps.
- However, motivation can fluctuate over time, especially when facing obstacles or monotony. Sustained motivation is key to maintaining consistency in your habits.
- Because motivation can waver, having strategies to boost and sustain it is essential for long-term success.

Understanding Your Sources of Motivation

- **Intrinsic Motivation:** This comes from within and is driven by personal satisfaction, enjoyment, or a sense of growth. For example, exercising because it makes you feel good and healthy.
- **Extrinsic Motivation:** This is driven by external rewards, recognition, or validation. Examples include earning a reward for completing a task or receiving praise from others.
- Identifying what truly motivates you—whether it's intrinsic, extrinsic, or a mix of both—can help you stay committed and create more effective strategies to maintain your habits.

Image Suggestion: A heart and a trophy icon representing intrinsic and extrinsic motivation.

Strategies to Sustain Motivation

- **Set Milestones:** Break your larger goals into smaller, more achievable steps. Each milestone you reach gives a sense of accomplishment, which fuels further motivation.
- **Celebrate Progress:** Reward yourself when you hit milestones. Celebrating small wins keeps the journey enjoyable and encourages you to keep moving forward.

- **Visualize Success:** Keep a clear picture of your goals and the benefits they bring. Visualization helps remind you of why the habit matters, boosting your motivation.
- **Stay Connected:** Engage with a supportive community or find a mentor. Sharing your progress with others can provide encouragement and accountability.

Why it matters?

Motivation is the engine that drives your habits forward. While initial enthusiasm can ignite action, learning to sustain motivation ensures long-term success. By tapping into intrinsic and extrinsic motivators, you create a compelling reason to keep going even when progress feels slow. Motivation keeps your goals alive, turning mundane actions into meaningful steps toward transformation. It helps you stay focused, optimistic, and committed to your growth journey, making it the key to achieving lasting change

Inspiring Thoughts to Reflect On

"People often say that motivation doesn't last. Well, neither does bathing—that's why we recommend it daily." – Zig Ziglar.

Ziglar, an influential American motivational speaker and author, was known for his humorous yet practical approach to personal growth. His teachings emphasized the importance of consistent effort and daily motivation to achieve lasting success. Swiss psychiatrist and psychoanalyst Carl Jung, a pioneer in analytical psychology said something similar. He emphasized the value of actions over intentions in shaping one's character. His insights into human behavior underline the profound connection between what we repeatedly do and who we ultimately become. He said –

"You are what you do, not what you say you'll do."

2.2.2. Mission 2 Day 2 Worksheet:

Instruction: This worksheet helps you clarify your motivation and design a system that keeps you inspired throughout your habit-building journey. Plan your rewards and accountability measures to maintain momentum, even when motivation fades.

Worksheet Sections:

Part 1: Defining Your Motivation

1. What's your primary motivation for building this habit?

   _____

   _____

   _____

2. How can you make your habit more meaningful and aligned with your values?

   _____

   _____

   _____

Part 2: Designing Your Motivation System

1. What small wins and rewards will you use to stay motivated?

   _____

   _____

   _____

   _____

   _____

2. What accountability measures will you put in place (e.g., sharing progress with a friend)?

_____

_____

_____

Part 3: Adjusting When Motivation Fades

1. How will you revisit your "why" if motivation dips?

_____

_____

_____

_____

2. What new routines or tweaks can you introduce to keep the habit interesting?

_____

_____

_____

_____

_____

2.2.3. Sample filled-up Worksheet for a Disciplined Person:

Part 1: Defining Your Motivation

1. What's your primary motivation for building this habit?

My primary motivation for building this habit is to enhance my productivity and overall well-being. Establishing this habit will help me achieve my long-term goals, improve my daily routines, and maintain a balanced and fulfilling lifestyle.

2. How can you make your habit more meaningful and aligned with your values?

To make this habit more meaningful, I will align it with my core values of personal growth and commitment to excellence. By integrating this habit into my daily routine and reflecting on its impact on my personal development, I can stay connected to its purpose. Additionally, I will set specific, value-driven goals that relate directly to my long-term vision and aspirations.

Part 2: Designing Your Motivation System

1. What small wins and rewards will you use to stay motivated?

- **Small Wins:** Completing mission milestones such as finishing a certain number of tasks or maintaining consistency for a mission.
- **Rewards:** Treating myself to a favourite activity, like watching a movie or enjoying a special meal, after achieving a milestone. I will also use non-material rewards like taking time for a relaxing hobby or enjoying a day off.

2. What accountability measures will you put in place (e.g., sharing progress with a friend)?

- **Accountability Partner:** I will share my progress with a trusted friend who is also working on building habits. We will have regular check-ins to discuss our successes and challenges.
- **Tracking System:** I will use a habit tracker app to monitor my daily progress and review it Monthly to assess my adherence and make necessary adjustments.
- **Public Commitment:** I will announce my goal on social media to create a sense of accountability and gain support from my network.

Part 3: Adjusting When Motivation Fades

1. How will you revisit your "why" if motivation dips?

I will revisit my "why" by regularly reviewing my initial reasons for starting this habit and reflecting on how it aligns with my long-term goals. I will keep a journal where I write about my progress, challenges, and the benefits I've experienced. This will help me reconnect with my purpose and reignite my motivation.

2. What new routines or tweaks can you introduce to keep the habit interesting?

- **Variety:** Introduce new elements or variations to my routine to keep it engaging. For example, if my habit is exercise, I could try different workout styles or locations.
- **Challenges:** Set mini-challenges or goals to achieve within a set period, such as increasing the intensity or duration of my routine.
- **Learning:** Incorporate new learning opportunities related to my habit, such as reading articles or watching videos that offer fresh perspectives and tips.

2.2.4. Sample filled-up Worksheet for a Struggling Person:

Part 1: Defining Your Motivation

1. What's your primary motivation for building this habit?

I want to build a habit of studying regularly because I know it's crucial for improving my health and toning up fitness. I feel like I'm falling behind in my workout sessions, and I need to catch up to avoid pending targets and improve my overall performance.

2. How can you make your habit more meaningful and aligned with your values?

To make studying more meaningful, I can connect it to my long-term goals, such as getting a healthy body and increasing to gain a healthy weight I'm passionate about. I can remind myself that each workout session brings me closer to achieving these goals and that it's an investment in my future. Additionally, setting specific, achievable goals for each gym session can help me see progress and stay motivated.

Part 2: Designing Your Motivation System

1. What small wins and rewards will you use to stay motivated?

- **Small Wins:** Completing a workout session, finishing a exercise, or understanding a difficult task.
- **Rewards:** Allowing myself to eat a favourite food or spend time on social media after a productive gym session. Also, treating myself to a small snack or taking a short break to relax can serve as immediate rewards.

2. What accountability measures will you put in place (e.g., sharing progress with a friend)?

- **Workout Group:** Joining or forming a body goals group with classmates to share progress and keep each other accountable.
- **Accountability Partner:** Regularly updating a friend or family member or journal on my health progress and goals.
- **Tracking Progress:** Using a study planner or app to track my workout hours and achievements and reviewing it mission-wise to assess my progress.

Part 3: Adjusting When Motivation Fades

1. How will you revisit your "why" if motivation dips?

I will remind myself of my long-term goals and the reasons why I want to improve my grades. Reflecting on the stress and frustration I felt before starting this habit can also help me stay focused. I'll create a vision board or a list of personal reasons and goals to keep visible, so I can see them whenever I feel my motivation waning.

2. What new routines or tweaks can you introduce to keep the habit interesting?

- **Variety:** Changing my work or gym environment or using different methods to keep things fresh and engaging.
- **Incorporate Interests:** Integrating workouts, I find particularly interesting or relevant to my gym sessions to make them more enjoyable.
- **Gamify Workout Sessions:** Turning body goals into small challenges or games with rewards for meeting milestones to make working out more fun.

2.3. Mission 2 Day 3: Resilience Building

2.3.1. Theory:

Resilience is vital in the habit-building process for several reasons. First, it helps you stick with habits when they become difficult or tedious. There will be moments of resistance or failure, and resilience provides the strength to keep going, even when results aren't immediate. Second, it allows you to recover from setbacks. Whether it's a missed workout, a break in a study habit, or a slip in a healthy diet, resilience helps you view these failures not as the end of your progress but as temporary hiccups. Finally, building resilience contributes to mental and emotional strength. When you practice resilience, you develop a growth mindset that sees challenges as opportunities to improve rather than threats.

Strategies to Build Resilience

1. **Embrace Setbacks:** Instead of seeing setbacks as failures, view them as learning experiences. When something doesn't go as planned, reflect on what happened and how you can adjust your approach. This perspective shifts your mindset from self-criticism to constructive problem-solving.

2. **Practice Self-Compassion:** Being kind to yourself during tough times is crucial. Acknowledge that building habits is hard work, and it's normal to encounter difficulties. Practising self-compassion allows you to accept mistakes without judgment and continue working toward your goals.

3. **Focus on Progress:** Recognize and celebrate small wins. Building habits is a gradual process, and acknowledging your efforts, no matter how small, keeps you motivated. Celebrating progress, rather than aiming for perfection, reinforces positive behaviour and strengthens your commitment.

4. **Stay Flexible:** Life is unpredictable, and sticking rigidly to a plan can lead to frustration when things don't go as expected. Being flexible with your habits allows you to adapt your approach and find solutions that work in different situations.

Practical Example: Building Resilience

Imagine you're struggling to stick to a study schedule. You set a goal to study for two hours daily, but distractions, low motivation, or unexpected commitments keep derailing your plans. Building resilience involves reflecting on why this schedule is challenging, identifying obstacles, and adjusting your strategy. You might decide to break the two-hour session into shorter, more manageable segments or find a different study environment.

Why it matters?

Resilience is your ability to bounce back from setbacks and continue moving forward. It is a cornerstone of personal growth, enabling you to stay consistent with your habits even when life gets tough. Building resilience empowers you to face challenges with confidence, adapt to change, and maintain focus on your goals. This strength not only supports your habit-building journey but also enhances your overall well-being and ability to handle life's uncertainties. Resilience ensures that temporary failures never derail your long-term progress

Inspiring Thoughts to Reflect On

"Do not judge me by my success. Judge me by how many times I fell down and got back up again," said Nelson Mandela, the renowned South African leader and anti-apartheid revolutionary who exemplified resilience and dedication to justice. His legacy of perseverance inspires people worldwide, echoing the same enduring strength found in Ralph Waldo Emerson's words:

"What lies behind us and what lies before us are tiny matters compared to what lies within us."

Emerson, an influential American philosopher and essayist, championed the power of inner strength and self-reliance, reminding us that true purpose and resilience come from within.

2.3.2. Mission 2 Day 3 Worksheet:

Instruction: Assess your current resilience and develop strategies to stay strong in the face of setbacks. Use this worksheet to plan how you'll bounce back quickly from disruptions and stay on track with your habits.

Worksheet Sections:

Part 1: Assessing Your Resilience

1. How well do you handle setbacks and challenges?

   _____
   _____
   _____

2. What's your usual response when your routine is disrupted?

   _____
   _____
   _____

Part 2: Building Resilience Strategies

1. What daily practices (e.g., affirmations, self-care) can boost your mental toughness?

   _____
   _____
   _____

2. How can you build a support system that helps during tough times?

_____
_____
_____

Part 3: Planning for Setbacks

1. What are the biggest triggers that lead to setbacks?

_____
_____
_____

2. What specific actions can you take to recover quickly when a setback happens?

_____
_____
_____

For more resources, follow step-by-step:
- Scan the QR-code
- Register/Login Using Email-Id or Phone No.
- Browse through course videos
- Access Feeds for daily motivational & tricks for habit transformation

2.3.3. Sample filled-up Worksheet for a Disciplined Person:

Part 1: Assessing Your Resilience
1. **How well do you handle setbacks and challenges?**
    - I generally handle setbacks quite well. When faced with challenges, I take a step back to assess the situation, identify what went wrong, and look for ways to improve. I try to stay calm and avoid negative self-talk, focusing instead on the lessons I can learn from each experience.

2. **What's your usual response when your routine is disrupted?**
    - When my routine is disrupted, I usually take a moment to reflect and re-evaluate my priorities. I identify what caused the disruption and make adjustments to my schedule or approach. I don't dwell on the setback for too long; instead, I focus on how to get back on track as soon as possible.

Part 2: Building Resilience Strategies
1. **What daily practices (e.g., affirmations, self-care) can boost your mental toughness?**
    - I practice daily affirmations in the morning, such as reminding myself of my goals and capabilities. I also include self-care routines like meditation and physical exercise to boost my mental and physical resilience. Journaling in the evening helps me reflect on the day's events, process any setbacks, and plan for a stronger tomorrow.

2. **How can you build a support system that helps during tough times?**
    - I can build a support system by sharing my goals with close friends or family members who can hold me accountable. Additionally, joining study groups or online communities with like-minded individuals can provide encouragement and motivation. I will also make it a habit to regularly check in with my support system to discuss progress and setbacks.

Part 3: Planning for Setbacks

1. **What are the biggest triggers that lead to setbacks?**
   - The biggest triggers include unexpected changes in my schedule, stress from other commitments, and feeling overwhelmed by the size of my goals. Sometimes, negative self-talk can also undermine my motivation, leading to setbacks.

2. **What specific actions can you take to recover quickly when a setback happens?**
   - When a setback occurs, I can take a few deep breaths and remind myself that setbacks are a natural part of the process. I will revisit my goals and break them down into smaller, manageable tasks to regain focus. Engaging in a brief self-care activity, like a 5-minute meditation or a quick walk, can help clear my mind and re-energize me to tackle the next steps.

2.3.4. Sample filled-up Worksheet for a Struggling Person:

Part 1: Assessing Your Resilience

1. **How well do you handle setbacks and challenges?**
   - I struggle a lot when setbacks happen. It often makes me feel demotivated, and I find it difficult to get back on track. I tend to get stuck in negative thinking and sometimes give up on my habits entirely.

2. **What's your usual response when your routine is disrupted?**
   - I usually become very frustrated and overwhelmed. My first reaction is to abandon the habit or routine for a while. It feels like I've failed, and I tell myself that maybe I'm not capable of sticking to it.

Part 2: Building Resilience Strategies
1. **What daily practices (e.g., affirmations, self-care) can boost your mental toughness?**
    - o I can start with simple affirmations like, "It's okay to have setbacks; what matters is trying again." Also, dedicating a few minutes each day to journaling my thoughts might help me process my feelings. Including small self-care practices, like taking a short walk, could help me clear my mind when things go wrong.
2. **How can you build a support system that helps during tough times?**
    - o I could talk to a close friend or family member and let them know about my goals. Asking them to check in with me occasionally might keep me accountable. Joining a support group or finding an online community related to my habit would also give me a sense of belonging and support.

Part 3: Planning for Setbacks
1. **What are the biggest triggers that lead to setbacks?**
    - o Feeling overwhelmed, lack of time, and self-doubt are my biggest triggers. When I get too busy or feel like I'm not making progress fast enough, I lose motivation.
2. **What specific actions can you take to recover quickly when a setback happens?**
    - o I can remind myself that setbacks are a normal part of any journey. When I face a setback, I will take a short break to breathe and regroup. I will review my goals, break them into smaller steps, and try to resume with a simpler version of my routine. Reaching out to my support system to talk about the setback might also help me regain focus.

2.4. Mission 2 Day 4: Consistency Planning

2.4.1. Theory:

Consistency is the driving force behind lasting habit change. While motivation can kick-start a habit, consistency sustains and solidifies it. When you show up every day, even in small ways, you lay the foundation for long-term success. Let's explore how consistency works and how to stay on track.

The Power of Consistency

- **Consistency is the repeated application of effort over time.** Building a habit isn't about doing something perfectly once; it's about showing up regularly, regardless of how small the action is. Over time, these small actions compound into meaningful change.

- **It builds momentum, making habits easier to maintain.** Each consistent action builds on the last, creating momentum that makes it easier to keep the habit going.

- **Small, consistent actions lead to big results.** Success isn't about drastic changes but about the cumulative impact of many small, steady steps.

Challenges to Maintaining Consistency

- A lack of immediate results can lead to slow progress.

- Life is unpredictable, and interruptions can break the rhythm of a habit. The key is to return to the habit as soon as possible.

- Doing the same thing done repeatedly can become dull, making it tempting to give up. Finding ways to keep the habit interesting is essential.

Strategies to Stay Consistent

- **Set Realistic Expectations: Understand that change takes time.** Start small and allow yourself to progress gradually.

- **Develop Routines: Make your habits part of your daily life.** Integrate your habit into your daily schedule so that it becomes automatic.

- **Use Reminders: Keep yourself on track with cues and alerts.** Use alarms, sticky notes, or habit-tracking apps to stay mindful of your habits.

- **Reward Consistency: Celebrate sticking to your habits.** Recognizing your effort can motivate you to keep going.

Why it matters?

Consistency is the backbone of habit formation and personal growth. By creating a structured plan to maintain regularity, you increase the likelihood of success. Consistency ensures that small, repeated efforts compound into significant results over time. It reduces the need for constant decision-making, turning habits into automatic behaviors. With a solid consistency plan, you align your actions with your goals, making growth inevitable. This focus transforms fleeting motivation into enduring progress, enabling you to achieve more with less effort

Inspiring Thoughts to Reflect On

"It's not what we do once in a while that shapes our lives. It's what we do consistently," says Tony Robbins, a world-renowned life coach and author known for his impactful work in personal development and peak performance. His teachings emphasize the transformative power of daily actions, mirroring the insights of John C. Maxwell, who states,

"Small disciplines repeated with consistency every day lead to great achievements gained slowly over time."

Maxwell, an influential leadership expert and speaker, advocates for steady progress and commitment as the keys to achieving lasting success, underscoring that greatness is built one disciplined step at a time.

For more resources, follow step-by-step:

- Scan the QR-code
- Register/Login Using Email-Id or Phone No.
- Browse through course videos
- Access Feeds for daily motivational & tricks for habit transformation

2.4.2. Mission 2 Day 4 Worksheet:

Instruction: This worksheet is designed to help you stay consistent with your key habits by planning small daily actions and tracking your progress. Reflect on potential challenges and make adjustments to maintain consistency.

Worksheet Sections:

Part 1: Identifying Key Habits

1. What are the top 3 habits you need to be consistent with daily?

   _____
   _____
   _____

2. How can you make these habits easier to complete every day?

   _____
   _____
   _____

Part 2: Planning for Consistency

1. What small actions can you take daily to maintain consistency?

   _____
   _____
   _____
   _____
   _____

2. What will you do if you miss a day to quickly get back on track?

_____

_____

_____

Part 3: Tracking and Adjusting

1. How will you track your daily habit performance?

   _____

   _____

   _____

2. What adjustments can you make if consistency is difficult?

   _____

   _____

   _____

2.4.3. Sample filled-up Worksheet for a Disciplined Person:

Part 1: Identifying Key Habits

1. **What are the top 3 habits you need to be consistent with daily?**
   - **Habit 1:** Studying for 1 hour.
   - **Habit 2:** Exercising for 30 minutes.
   - **Habit 3:** Reading a self-improvement book for 20 minutes.

2. **How can you make these habits easier to complete every day?**
   - **Studying:** Set a fixed study schedule and prepare all materials the night before to avoid delays.
   - **Exercising:** Lay out workout clothes and equipment in advance and create a playlist to keep motivation high.
   - **Reading:** Keep the book on my bedside table and read right before bed as part of my nighttime routine.

Part 2: Planning for Consistency

1. **What small actions can you take daily to maintain consistency?**
   - For **studying**, start with a 5-minute review of previous material to get into the right mindset.
   - For **exercising**, do a 5-minute warm-up every morning to trigger the start of the workout.
   - For **reading**, I sct a reminder on my phone and use a bookmark to keep track of progress.

2. **What will you do if you miss a day to quickly get back on track?**
   - Acknowledge the missed day without judgment. The next day, double the focus on the habit, like adding an extra 10 minutes to the study session or exercise routine to make up for it.

Part 3: Tracking and Adjusting

1. **How will you track your daily habit performance?**
   - Use a dedicated planner or habit tracker app to mark each completed habit daily. I will also write a brief reflection in a

journal on how I felt about my performance to monitor my progress.

2. **What adjustments can you make if consistency is difficult?**

    o **Studying:** Break the 1-hour session into two 30-minute segments if maintaining focus for the full hour is challenging.

    o **Exercising:** Swap a high-intensity workout for a 30-minute walk if feeling physically or mentally drained.

    o **Reading:** Switch to a different self-improvement book if I'm losing interest, ensuring the habit remains enjoyable and engaging.

2.4.4. Sample filled-up Worksheet for a Struggling Person:

Part 1: Identifying Key Habits

1. **What are the top 3 habits you need to be consistent with daily?**

    o **Habit 1:** Studying for at least 30 minutes.

    o **Habit 2:** Drinking 8 glasses of water.

    o **Habit 3:** Practicing mindfulness for 5 minutes.

2. **How can you make these habits easier to complete every day?**

    o **Studying:** Set up a designated study space with all materials ready and keep the sessions short.

    o **Drinking Water:** Keep a water bottle within arm's reach and set reminders on my phone every hour.

    o **Mindfulness:** Use a guided meditation app to help stay focused for the 5-minute practice.

Part 2: Planning for Consistency

1. **What small actions can you take daily to maintain consistency?**

    o For **studying**, break down tasks into smaller chunks, like reading 5 pages or summarizing a concept.

    o For **drinking water**, I take a sip of water every time I complete a task or transition between activities.

    o For **mindfulness**, use the 5-minute timer on the app to keep it manageable and achievable.

2. **What will you do if you miss a day to quickly get back on track?**
   - Remind myself that one missed day doesn't mean failure. The next day, I'll set a smaller, more achievable goal (e.g., study for just 10 minutes) to ease back into the habit.

Part 3: Tracking and Adjusting

1. **How will you track your daily habit performance?**
   - Use a simple habit tracker app to log each habit daily and mark them off when completed. I will also keep a notebook where I write a quick sentence about how I felt while completing the habit.
   - I can use alarm clock to remind me of the works I have to do in a particular day.

2. **What adjustments can you make if consistency is difficult?**
   - **Studying:** Reduce the time to 15 minutes if 30 minutes feels too overwhelming.
   - **Drinking Water:** Add flavour to the water (like lemon or mint) to make it more enjoyable.
   - **Mindfulness:** Switch to deep breathing exercises if guided meditation feels too challenging some days.

For more resources, follow step-by-step:
- Scan the QR-code
- Register/Login Using Email-Id or Phone No.
- Browse through course videos
- Access Feeds for daily motivational & tricks for habit transformation

2.5. Mission 2 Day 5: Accountability

2.5.1. Theory:

Accountability is a powerful tool in habit formation. It involves being responsible to someone else for your actions, decisions, and progress. When we have someone to report to or share our journey with, the likelihood of sticking to our habits increases significantly. It creates a sense of external motivation and pressure that helps us stay on track. Unlike self-motivation, which can wane over time, accountability taps into our social instincts, making us more committed and focused.

The Role of Accountability in Habit Formation

- Accountability helps us remain consistent by providing **external motivation** and a sense of responsibility.
- It enhances our **commitment** to habits, as sharing our goals with others makes them feel more concrete.
- When we know that someone is monitoring our progress, we are more likely to follow through on our actions and push through challenges.

Types of Accountability Partners

1. **Peer Accountability:** This involves partnering with someone who shares similar goals. It fosters a mutual sense of support and understanding, as both individuals are on a similar journey.

2. **Mentorship Accountability:** Receiving guidance and feedback from a mentor or coach can be highly effective. Mentors can provide valuable insights, strategies, and motivation based on their experience.

3. **Group Accountability:** Being part of a group or community creates a network of support. In group settings, shared experiences and encouragement can be key drivers of success.

How to Find and Engage Accountability Partners

- **Choose someone you trust and respect.** Trust builds openness, while respect ensures both parties take the process seriously.

- **Set clear expectations** for support and check-ins. This structure helps maintain focus and commitment.
- **Be open to feedback.** Constructive criticism is an essential aspect of growth and improvement.

Why it matters?

Accountability creates a powerful feedback loop that keeps you committed to your goals. Whether through self-monitoring or sharing progress with others, accountability ensures you stay on track even when motivation wanes. It fosters responsibility, builds trust, and strengthens your commitment to habit-building. Accountability partners or systems provide encouragement, guidance, and a sense of shared purpose, making the journey more manageable and rewarding. This step transforms your individual effort into a collaborative and effective growth strategy.

Inspiring Thoughts to Reflect On

"Accountability breeds response-ability,"

- noted Stephen Covey, the influential author of 'The 7 Habits of Highly Effective People', whose work focuses on personal integrity and the power of taking ownership of one's actions. Similarly, Oprah Winfrey, media mogul and philanthropist, encourages self-growth by advising,

"Surround yourself with people who hold you to a higher standard," underscoring the impact of supportive relationships on personal development. Thomas S. Monson, a prominent leader and speaker, reinforces this idea, asserting,

"When performance is measured, performance improves. When performance is measured and reported, the rate of improvement accelerates," highlighting the transformative power of accountability and structured feedback. Together, these insights reveal how responsibility and high standards drive sustained growth and improvement.

2.5.2. Mission 2 Day 5 Worksheet:

Instruction: Use this worksheet to establish a support system for staying on track with your habits. Identify your accountability needs, choose reliable partners, and create a structure for regular check-ins and feedback.

Worksheet Sections:

Part 1: Identifying Accountability Needs

1. Which habits do you need support with to stay consistent?

   _____
   _____
   _____

2. What type of accountability system will work best for you (peer, public, technology)?

   _____
   _____
   _____

Part 2: Choosing Accountability Partners

1. Who/what can help hold you accountable and support your habit goals?

   _____
   _____
   _____
   _____

2. How will you establish a routine for regular check-ins and feedback?

___

Part 3: Planning Your Accountability Structure

1. What will your check-ins look like (frequency, format)?

___

2. How will you track and share progress with your accountability partner?

___

2.5.3. Sample filled-up Worksheet for a Disciplined Person:

Part 1: Identifying Accountability Needs

1. **Which habits do you need support with to stay consistent?**
   - Daily exercise routine.
   - Reading at least 30 minutes each day.
   - Following a balanced diet plan.

2. **What type of accountability system will work best for you (peer, public, technology)?**
   - A **peer accountability** system will work best for me. Having a friend or family member check in with me regularly can provide the support I need.
   - Additionally, I will use **technology**, like a habit-tracking app, to monitor my progress daily.

Part 2: Choosing Accountability Partners

1. **Who can help hold you accountable and support your habit goals?**
   - My best friend, who also wants to adopt similar habits, can be my accountability partner.
   - Additionally, I will involve my family members to check in on my diet plan as they share meals with me.

2. **How will you establish a routine for regular check-ins and feedback?**
   - I will schedule a mission-based check-in every Sunday evening with my accountability partner to discuss my progress.
   - For daily habits, we will send each other a brief message at the end of each day to confirm completion.

Part 3: Planning Your Accountability Structure

1. **What will your check-ins look like (frequency, format)?**
   - **Mission check-ins:** Video calls every Sunday evening to review the mission's progress, discuss any challenges, and plan for the upcoming mission.
   - **Daily check-ins:** A quick message or voice note to confirm if the daily habits were completed.

2. **How will you track and share progress with your accountability partner?**
   - I will use a habit-tracking app to log daily activities and share screenshots of my progress for each mission.
   - We will also keep a shared Google Doc to note down mission-based reflections and any adjustments needed.

2.5.4. Sample filled-up Worksheet for a Struggling Person:

Part 1: Identifying Accountability Needs

1. **Which habits do you need support with to stay consistent?**
   - I struggle with staying consistent in my exercise routine and following a healthy diet. I also need support in sticking to my daily study schedule.

2. **What type of accountability system will work best for you (peer, public, technology)?**
   - A peer system might be helpful, but I worry about burdening others. Public accountability feels too intense, so perhaps using a simple app for tracking might be more manageable.

Part 2: Choosing Accountability Partners

1. **Who can help hold you accountable and support your habit goals?**
   - I could ask my best friend to check in on me once a mission. I also have a family member who has been through similar struggles and might understand my challenges.

2. **How will you establish a routine for regular check-ins and feedback?**

- I'll aim for a casual check-in with my friend every Friday. We can keep it short, but just a quick text or call to go over how my mission went. I might also try setting reminders on my phone.

Part 3: Planning Your Accountability Structure
1. **What will your check-ins look like (frequency, format)?**
    - Once a mission, either via text or a short phone call. If that feels too much, maybe we can adjust it to every other mission.
2. **How will you track and share progress with your accountability partner?**
    - I'll use a simple habit-tracking app to log my daily progress. During our check-ins, I'll share a screenshot of the mission's progress, even if it's not perfect. This will help keep me honest about my efforts.

For more resources, follow step-by-step:
- Scan the QR-code
- Register/Login Using Email-Id or Phone No.
- Browse through course videos
- Access Feeds for daily motivational & tricks for habit transformation

2.6. Mission 2 Day 6: Habit Stacking

2.6.1. Theory:

Habit stacking is a powerful technique for adding new habits into your daily routine. It involves linking a new habit to an existing one, using the established routine as a trigger for the new behaviour. By piggybacking on something you already do consistently, you reduce the mental effort needed to adopt a new habit, making it easier to stick with over time.

What is Habit Stacking?

Habit stacking connects a new habit to an already ingrained one. The concept is simple: you identify a habit you already perform every day and then add a new, desired habit to that routine. For example, if you have a habit of brushing your teeth in the morning, you could use that as a trigger to meditate for five minutes afterwards. This way, the new habit is 'stacked' on top of the existing one, creating a smooth flow of activities.

Benefits of Habit Stacking

- **Builds on Established Routines:** Since the new habit is linked to a routine you already follow; it becomes easier to integrate into your day.
- **Creates a Natural Flow:** Habit stacking helps create a sequence of actions, making your day feel more structured and organized.
- **Reduces Effort:** By tying the new habit to a familiar one, you minimize the effort needed to adopt new behaviours. This is because the existing habit acts as a cue, triggering the new habit naturally.

How to Stack Habits Effectively

1. **Start with a Strong Habit:** Choose an existing habit that you do consistently, such as drinking coffee in the morning.
2. **Align with Your Goals:** Pick a new habit that aligns with your personal or professional goals.
3. **Keep it Small:** Begin with a small, manageable habit to avoid feeling overwhelmed.
4. **Gradual Growth:** As the new habit becomes part of your routine, gradually increase its complexity or duration.

Example: If your existing habit is drinking coffee every morning, you could use that time to write down three things you're grateful for. This creates a positive morning ritual that is easy to maintain.

Why it matters?

Habit stacking simplifies habit formation by anchoring new behaviors to existing routines. This strategy leverages the momentum of current habits, making it easier to adopt positive changes. By connecting habits, you create seamless sequences that require less mental effort to maintain. Habit stacking amplifies your productivity, helping you build powerful routines that align with your goals. It's a practical and effective way to integrate growth into your daily life, ensuring consistent and sustainable progress.

Inspiring Thoughts to Reflect On

Warren Buffett, one of the world's most successful investors, emphasizes the importance of habits in shaping our lives with his quote,

"Chains of habit are too light to be felt until they are too heavy to be broken."

Known for his disciplined approach to investing, Buffett highlights how small, seemingly insignificant habits accumulate over time, eventually becoming powerful forces. Similarly, Vincent Van Gogh, the iconic Dutch painter, expressed a similar belief in the power of consistent effort, stating,

"Great things are not done by impulse but by a series of small things brought together."

Van Gogh's mastery of art was the result of countless small, deliberate actions and improvements. Both quotes reflect the importance of consistent effort and the impact of small actions over time in achieving lasting success.

2.6.2. Mission 2 Day 6 Worksheet:

Instruction: This worksheet guides you in linking new habits to existing routines through habit stacking. Plan a simple, actionable habit stack and adjust it as needed to fit smoothly into your daily schedule.

Worksheet Sections:

Part 1: Identifying Routine Anchors

1. What are consistent daily routines or actions you already perform?

   _____

   _____

   _____

   _____

   _____

2. How can you use these anchors to introduce new habits?

   _____

   _____

   _____

   _____

Part 2: Designing Your Habit Stack

1. What habit do you want to stack onto your existing routine?

   _____

   _____

   _____

2. How can you make the stacked habit small, simple, and easy to complete?

_____

_____

_____

Part 3: Tracking and Adjusting Your Stack

1. How will you measure the success of your habit stack?

_____

_____

_____

2. What tweaks can you make if the stack doesn't work smoothly?

_____

_____

_____

2.6.3. Sample filled-up Worksheet for a Disciplined Person:

Part 1: Identifying Routine Anchors

1. **What are consistent daily routines or actions you already perform?**
   - I brush my teeth every morning.
   - I drink a cup of coffee at breakfast.
   - I check my emails when I start work.
   - I take a walk after lunch.
   - I read a book before going to bed.

2. **How can you use these anchors to introduce new habits?**
   - I can introduce a short meditation session right after brushing my teeth.
   - While having my morning coffee, I can write down three things I'm grateful for.
   - After checking my emails, I can set my top three priorities for the day.
   - During my lunch walk, I can listen to an educational podcast.
   - Before reading a book at night, I can reflect on the day and note my achievements.

Part 2: Designing Your Habit Stack

1. **What habit do you want to stack onto your existing routine?**
   - I want to stack a short 5-minute meditation session onto my morning routine right after brushing my teeth.

2. **How can you make the stacked habit small, simple, and easy to complete?**
   - I will start with just 2 minutes of breathing exercises to make it simple and gradually increase the duration as it becomes a natural part of my routine.

Part 3: Tracking and Adjusting Your Stack

1. **How will you measure the success of your habit stack?**

   o   I will track my progress using a daily habit tracker app and mark each day I complete my meditation session. I'll also note how I feel after meditating to see if it positively affects my day.

2. **What tweaks can you make if the stack doesn't work smoothly?**

   o   If I find it challenging to meditate immediately after brushing my teeth, I could try stacking it onto my coffee routine instead. I will keep adjusting the timing until it becomes a consistent habit.

2.6.4. Sample filled-up Worksheet for a Struggling Person:

Part 1: Identifying Routine Anchors

1. **What are consistent daily routines or actions you already perform?**

   o   I brush my teeth every morning.
   o   I drink coffee before starting work.
   o   I scroll through my phone right before bed.

2. **How can you use these anchors to introduce new habits?**

   o   I could try adding a 1-minute deep breathing exercise right after brushing my teeth.
   o   While drinking my coffee, I can take a few moments to plan my day.
   o   Before scrolling through my phone at night, I can try writing down one positive thing that happened during the day.

Part 2: Designing Your Habit Stack

1. **What habit do you want to stack onto your existing routine?**

   o   I want to add a short gratitude practice before scrolling through my phone at night.

2. **How can you make the stacked habit small, simple, and easy to complete?**
   - I will keep it as simple as writing just one thing I am grateful for in a notebook by my bed. It shouldn't take more than 30 seconds.

Part 3: Tracking and Adjusting Your Stack

1. **How will you measure the success of your habit stack?**
   - I'll use a simple calendar where I can mark an "X" on each day that I write down my gratitude. This way, I can see how often I'm following through.

2. **What tweaks can you make if the stack doesn't work smoothly?**
   - If I keep forgetting, I might set a reminder on my phone or move my notebook to a spot I'll definitely see when I pick up my phone at night. If writing feels too difficult, I might start by just thinking about one thing I'm grateful for instead.

For more resources, follow step-by-step:

- Scan the QR-code
- Register/Login Using Email-Id or Phone No.
- Browse through course videos
- Access Feeds for daily motivational & tricks for habit transformation

2.7. Mission 2 Day 7: Mission 2 Reflection

2.7.1. Theory:

Reflecting on your progress helps you identify effective strategies and areas needing improvement. Celebrating your achievements keeps you motivated, and preparing for the next mission ensures continued progress and success.

Start by considering the obstacles you faced during the mission. What challenges did you encounter, and how did you tackle them? This reflection helps you understand what strategies worked and what didn't. For instance, if you struggled with staying motivated, think about what specific factors contributed to this struggle and how you addressed them.

Next, evaluate how you maintained motivation throughout the mission. Did you use any particular techniques or reminders that kept you going? Recognize the habits you managed to stick with and identify those that need more attention. Perhaps you were consistent with your morning routine but found it harder to maintain your evening habits.

Reflect on how the concepts of accountability and habit stacking played a role in your mission. Did having an accountability partner or using habit-stacking techniques help you stay on track? Consider whether these methods were effective or if adjustments are needed.

Celebrating Wins:

It's important to celebrate the progress you've made. Take a moment to acknowledge the milestones you've achieved, no matter how small. These victories are stepping-stones towards your larger goals and contribute significantly to your long-term success. Recognize how these wins fit into your overall objectives and how they boost your confidence.

Preparing for the Next Mission:

Use what you've learned in this mission to set new goals. Based on your reflections, adjust your routines and strategies to better align with your objectives. This might mean refining your habit-stacking approach or finding new ways to stay motivated.

Stay committed to your journey and remember that each mission is an opportunity to build on your success. Keep focused on your goals and continue to apply the insights gained from this mission as you move forward.

Why it matters?

Reflection is the process of learning from your experiences and applying those insights to improve. By reviewing your progress, you gain a clear understanding of what worked, what didn't, and how to move forward. Reflection fosters self-awareness, ensuring that your habits remain aligned with your goals. It helps you celebrate successes, identify areas for improvement, and stay adaptable in your growth journey. Regular reflection transforms effort into wisdom, making it an indispensable part of lasting personal development.

Inspiring Thoughts to Reflect On

John Dewey, an influential American philosopher and educator, profoundly stated,

"We do not learn from experience... we learn from reflecting on experience."

Dewey believed that true learning occurs when individuals take the time to critically examine their experiences and adapt accordingly. This idea is echoed in the anonymous quote, *"Pause and remember—progress comes from reflection and adaptation,"* which highlights how reflection is key to improvement and growth. Peter Drucker, a renowned management consultant and author, further emphasized this idea, stating,

"Follow effective action with quiet reflection. From the quiet reflection will come even more effective action."

Drucker's perspective underscores that reflective thinking is essential to refining actions and achieving sustained success. All three quotes emphasize the critical role of reflection in personal and professional growth, suggesting that it is through thoughtful analysis that true progress is made.

2.7.2. Mission 2 Reflection Worksheet

Instruction: Reflect on your progress and evaluate which habit strategies worked best for this mission. Use this worksheet to identify areas for improvement and set goals for the next phase of your habit journey.

Worksheet Sections:

Part 1: Reflecting on Your Progress

1. What were your biggest wins on this mission?

   _____

   _____

   _____

2. What challenges did you encounter, and how did you handle them?

   _____

   _____

   _____

Part 2: Evaluating Your Habit Strategies

1. Which strategies worked best for staying consistent and accountable?

   _____

   _____

   _____

   _____

2. What adjustments do you need to make going forward?

___

Part 3: Planning for the Next Mission

1. What habits do you want to continue building on the next mission?

___

2. What new challenges or goals will you focus on?

___

2.7.3. Sample filled-up Worksheet for a Disciplined Person:

Part 1: Reflecting on Progress

1. **What obstacles did you face, and how did you overcome them?**
   - **Obstacles:** I encountered challenges with maintaining consistency due to unexpected work demands and occasional lack of motivation.
   - **Solutions:** I addressed these obstacles by adjusting my schedule to allocate specific times for my new habits and using motivational reminders. I also reviewed my goals daily to stay focused.

2. **How did you stay motivated throughout the mission?**
   - I stayed motivated by setting clear, achievable goals and tracking my progress. I used positive reinforcement, such as rewarding myself for completing tasks, and stayed connected with my accountability partner for regular encouragement and feedback.

3. **What habits were you consistent with, and which ones need more focus?**
   - **Consistent Habits:** I was consistent with my morning exercise routine and daily journaling.
   - **Habits Needing Focus:** I need to improve consistency with my evening reading habits. I plan to adjust my bedtime to ensure I have time for reading each night.

4. **How did accountability and habit stacking help you?**
   - **Accountability:** Having a monthly check-in with my accountability partner provided the external motivation I needed to stay on track. It helped me stay committed and made me more aware of my progress.
   - **Habit Stacking:** Combining my new habit of meditating with an existing habit of drinking coffee made it easier to integrate the new practice into my daily routine without feeling overwhelmed.

Part 2: Celebrating Wins

1. **Identify and celebrate the progress you've made in this mission.**
   - I successfully integrated meditation into my morning routine and made progress in my fitness goals. Celebrating these wins by treating myself to a relaxing activity, like a movie night, helps reinforce my achievements.

2. **Acknowledge any milestones or small victories.**
   - Reaching my goal of exercising five times a mission and consistently journaling each day are significant milestones. I also achieved a personal best in my workout routine, which is a notable victory.

3. **Reflect on how these wins contribute to your long-term goals.**
   - These wins contribute to building a strong foundation for a healthier lifestyle and improved mental well-being. They reinforce my commitment to long-term goals of maintaining a balanced and productive daily routine.

Part 3: Preparing for the Next Mission

1. **Set new goals based on what you learned during this mission.**
   - For the next mission, my goals are to establish a more structured evening routine that includes dedicated reading time and to enhance my meditation practice by increasing its duration to 10 minutes.

2. **Adjust your routines and strategies as needed.**
   - I will adjust my evening routine by setting a specific time for reading and ensuring that it is incorporated into my schedule. Additionally, I will use habit stacking to link my meditation practice to my existing bedtime routine.

3. **Stay committed to your journey, and keep building on your success.**
   - I will stay committed by regularly reviewing my progress, maintaining open communication with my accountability partner, and celebrating my successes along the way. This approach will help me remain focused and motivated as I continue to develop positive habits.

2.7.4. Sample filled-up Worksheet for a Struggling Person:

Part 1: Reflecting on Progress

1. **What obstacles did you face, and how did you overcome them?**
    - o **Obstacles:** I struggled with sticking to my new habits due to a busy schedule and frequent distractions. I often forgot to complete tasks or didn't feel motivated to do them.
    - o **Solutions:** I tried setting reminders on my phone and creating a checklist, but I often ignored them or forgot to use them. I plan to find a more reliable way to stay on track, such as having a visible calendar.

2. **How did you stay motivated throughout the mission?**
    - o **Motivation:** I didn't stay very motivated for this mission. I found it hard to keep going, especially when I didn't see immediate results. I mostly relied on brief bursts of motivation from inspirational quotes, but they didn't always help.

3. **What habits were you consistent with, and which ones need more focus?**
    - o **Consistent Habits:** I managed to remember to brush my teeth and eat meals regularly, but I struggled with sticking to my new habits, like daily exercise and journaling.
    - o **Habits Needing Focus:** I need to focus more on integrating exercise and journaling into my daily routine. I missed several days and often felt overwhelmed.

4. **How did accountability and habit stacking help you?**
    - o **Accountability:** I had a hard time sticking to my accountability check-ins because I didn't always follow through with them. This lack of follow-through made it difficult to see the benefits of accountability.
    - o **Habit Stacking:** I attempted to stack journaling after brushing my teeth, but I forgot to do it some days. I need to find a better way to make this connection more automatic.

Part 2: Celebrating Wins

1. **Identify and celebrate the progress you've made in this mission.**
   - **Progress:** I completed some of my tasks, like remembering to brush my teeth and eat meals. I'm trying to celebrate these small wins by acknowledging them, even if they feel minor.
2. **Acknowledge any milestones or small victories.**
   - **Milestones:** I managed to stick with a few of my old habits without missing them entirely, which is a small victory. I need to recognize these as steps towards better consistency.
3. **Reflect on how these wins contribute to your long-term goals.**
   - **Contribution:** While my progress has been slow, these small wins helped build a foundation for future success. I see that even small achievements are important for building better habits over time.

Part 3: Preparing for the Next Mission

1. **Set new goals based on what you learned during this mission.**
   - **New Goals:** For the next mission, I'll set more realistic goals, like exercising twice a mission instead of daily. I'll also try to use a visible calendar or planner to remind me of my tasks.
2. **Adjust your routines and strategies as needed.**
   - **Adjustments:** I'll simplify my habit stack by choosing only one new habit to focus on for each mission. I'll make sure to set reminders and establish a clear routine to make it easier to follow through.
3. **Stay committed to your journey, and keep building on your success.**
   - **Commitment:** I'll try to stay committed by setting small, achievable goals and celebrating the progress I make, even if it's minor. I'll also seek more support and advice to help improve my consistency.

Chapter – 3

3.1. Mission 3 Day 1: Deepening Your Understanding of Cues

3.1.1. Theory:

Cues are the triggers that set off a habit. They can be subtle or very obvious, but their role in habit formation is crucial. By understanding cues, you can gain control over your habits—whether that means reinforcing good habits or breaking bad ones. There are four main types of cues:

1. **Environmental Cues:** These are external factors like location, objects, or even the weather that trigger a habit. For example, seeing a book on your bedside table might prompt you to read before sleeping. Consider how rearranging your environment can help promote positive habits.

2. **Temporal Cues:** These cues are related to time, such as specific times of the day or certain dates. An example might be checking your phone every morning at 7 AM when the alarm goes off. Recognizing temporal cues allows you to anchor new habits to existing routines, making them easier to adopt.

3. **Emotional Cues:** These are feelings that drive certain behaviours. Stress might lead you to eat comfort food, or excitement might make you want to call a friend. Understanding emotional cues can help you redirect energy from negative habits (like stress eating) to positive ones (like exercising).

4. **Social Cues:** These come from the influence of others, such as friends or social groups. You might find yourself joining a gym because your friends are doing so. Social cues can be powerful motivators; using them wisely can help build beneficial habits.

Practical Exercise:

Identify one habit you want to change or build. List all the possible cues (environmental, temporal, emotional, social) that trigger this habit. Create a cue map to visualize these connections. For example, if your habit is checking your phone in the morning, cues might include the sound of the alarm (temporal), the location of your phone (environmental), or a desire to see new messages (emotional).

Why it matters?

Cues are the triggers that initiate every habit. By deepening your understanding of these signals, you can better predict and control your behaviors. Identifying and analyzing cues allow you to disrupt negative patterns and create powerful opportunities for positive change. This knowledge helps you align your habits with your goals by intentionally designing your environment and responses. The ability to recognize and influence cues is a vital skill for mastering habit formation and ensuring long-term personal growth.

Inspiring Thoughts to Reflect On

"Triggers don't control you—they guide you. The power to act is yours."

James Clear, a bestselling author known for his expertise on habit formation and behavioral change, is celebrated for his book Atomic Habits. His quote,

"Every habit starts with a cue. Control the cue, and you control the habit," reflects his insights into the psychology of habits, where he emphasizes that by managing our environment and the cues around us, we can reshape our behavior patterns for lasting improvement. Clear's work offers a practical roadmap for building productive habits and breaking unhelpful ones through a focus on cues and intentional triggers.

3.1.2. Mission 3 Day 1 Worksheet:

Instruction: Use this worksheet to Reflect on how different cues influence your habits. Then, Complete the exercises below to identify your personal cues.

Worksheet Sections:

1. **Identify Cues in Your Daily Habits**

   List one habit you have and the cues that trigger it.

   - Habit: _____
   - Cues:
     a) Environmental: _____
     b) Temporal: _____
     c) Emotional: _____
     d) Social: _____

2. **Exercise: Cues Mapping**

   Draw a web connecting one habit with all the possible cues that trigger it.

   Example: Phone use -> Alarm sound, boredom, friend's message, lunch break.

3. **Fill in the Blanks**
    - Cues are important because they _____ _____.
    - One cue I often overlook is _____ _____.

4. **Personalization**
How can you adjust or add cues to better support one of your positive habits?

_____

_____

_____

_____

For more resources, follow step-by-step:
- Scan the QR-code
- Register/Login Using Email-Id or Phone No.
- Browse through course videos
- Access Feeds for daily motivational & tricks for habit transformation

3.1.3. Sample filled-up Worksheet for a Disciplined Person:

1. What are cues, and why are they important for habits?

- Cues are triggers that initiate habits. They can be subtle or obvious, such as environmental, temporal, emotional, or social cues. They are important because without them, habits wouldn't start automatically.

2. Exercise: Identify at least three cues for one of your habits.

- **Habit:** Going for a morning run.
    - **Environmental Cue:** My running shoes by the door.
    - **Temporal Cue:** 6:00 AM on my alarm.
    - **Emotional Cue:** The feeling of excitement to start the day fresh.

3. Fill in the blanks:

- A **temporal cue** might be a specific time, such as **7:00 AM**.
- An **emotional cue** could be feelings of **stress**, prompting me to meditate.

4. Action Plan:

- I will place my running shoes closer to the door to reinforce my morning running habit.
- I will set an alarm with a motivational message to increase the emotional impact of the cue.

Reflection:

- I've realized how much my habits are influenced by the environment, and I plan to use stronger cues to support my goals.

3.1.4. Sample filled-up Worksheet for a Struggling Person:

What are cues, and why are they important for habits?

- Cues are signals or triggers that start habits. I understand their importance, but I struggle to notice them in my own life. It's hard for me to recognize what triggers my bad habits.

2. Exercise: Identify at least three cues for one of your habits.

- **Habit:** Skipping breakfast and just grabbing coffee.
    - **Environmental Cue:** Rushing out the door.

- o **Temporal Cue:** 8:30 AM, when I realize I'm late for class.
- o **Emotional Cue:** Anxiety about being unprepared for the day.

3. Fill in the blanks:

- A temporal cue might be when I notice I'm running late.
- An emotional cue could be feelings of stress, prompting me to skip breakfast.

Action Plan:

- Honestly, I'm not sure how to fix this yet. I feel like everything's so rushed in the mornings. Maybe I could try prepping breakfast the night before, but I don't have the energy to plan ahead.

Reflection:

- I'm realizing that stress is a major driver of my bad habits. I need to work on managing my stress, but I don't know where to start.

For more resources, follow step-by-step:

- ↓ Scan the QR-code
- ↓ Register/Login Using Email-Id or Phone No.
- ↓ Browse through course videos
- ↓ Access Feeds for daily motivational & tricks for habit transformation

3.2. Mission 3 Day 2: Optimizing Routine Design

3.2.1. Theory:

Routines are the steps you take to execute a habit. A well-designed routine can help you build strong habits, while a poorly designed one can lead to failure. To optimize a routine, you need to ensure it is:

1. **Simple:** The simpler the routine, the easier it is to follow consistently. Complexity can lead to decision fatigue, which might cause you to abandon the routine altogether. For example, instead of planning a 1-hour workout, start with a 10-minute walk daily.

2. **Consistent:** Consistency is more important than intensity. A routine that can be done daily with little effort is more sustainable. Align your routine with regular daily activities. For instance, if you want to meditate, try doing it right after brushing your teeth in the morning.

3. **Aligned with Goals:** Your routine should support your long-term objectives. If your goal is to get fit, your routine should include exercise, balanced meals, and adequate sleep. When routines align with your broader goals, they become more meaningful and easier to maintain.

Practical Exercise: Take one of your existing routines and break it down into steps. Identify any areas where it could be simplified or where it doesn't align with your goals. For instance, if your morning routine involves checking emails first thing, consider replacing it with a quick workout or a 5-minute mindfulness practice.

Why it matters?

Your routines are the heart of your habits, determining the actions you take after a cue. Optimizing routines ensures that your behaviors are efficient, effective, and aligned with your goals. This process reduces friction, making it easier to stay consistent and achieve success. Well-designed routines save time, increase productivity, and prevent energy from being wasted on unnecessary decisions.

Inspiring Thoughts to Reflect On

As some unknown person said,
"A well-crafted routine turns effort into ease and chaos into clarity."

3.2.2. Mission 3 Day 2 Worksheet:

Instruction: This worksheet helps you to evaluate a current routine of yours and think of ways to improve it.

Worksheet Sections:

1. **Routine Breakdown**
   Write down one habit routine you perform regularly:

   o   Routine:

   _____

   _____

Now, identify the aspects that make it work:

   o   Simple: _____

   o   Consistent: _____

   o   Aligned with goals: _____

2. **Routine Optimization**
   List three ways you can simplify or adjust your routine to make it more effective:

   1. _____
   2. _____
   3. _____

3. **Fill in the Blanks**

   o   An effective routine should be _____ and _____.

   o   One common pitfall I face is _____.

4. **Exercise: Routine Mapping**
   Sketch a flowchart of your morning or evening routine. Where can you optimize or simplify?

3.2.3. Sample filled-up Worksheet for a Disciplined Person:

1. What are the key elements of an effective routine?
- Simplicity, consistency, and alignment with long-term goals. The routine should be easy to follow and regularly repeatable.

2. Exercise: Break down one of your routines into steps and optimize it.
- **Routine:** Evening study session.
    - Current Steps:
        1. Gather study materials.
        2. Read textbooks for an hour.
        3. Take a break after each hour.
        4. Write down notes before bed.
    - Optimized Routine:
        5. Gather materials the night before.
        6. Read in 30-minute segments to maintain focus.
        7. Take a 10-minute break between segments.
        8. Write notes immediately after studying to retain information better.

3. Fill in the blanks:
- Keeping routines **simple** and **consistent** makes them easier to follow.
- Adding a clear **reward** at the end of a routine increases motivation.

Action Plan:
- I will use a timer to keep my study sessions manageable and avoid long breaks that make it hard to resume.

Reflection:
Breaking my personal routine into smaller chunks makes it easier to stay focused. I feel more productive already.

3.2.4. Sample filled-up Worksheet for a Struggling Person:

What are the key elements of an effective routine?
- Routines are supposed to be simple and consistent, but I feel like every time I try to make one, I get off track because something unexpected happens, and I lose motivation.

2. Exercise: Break down one of your routines into steps and optimize it.
- **Routine:** Preparing a work report.
    - **Current Steps:**
        1. Find relevant materials.
        2. Get distracted by my phone.
        3. Work for 15 minutes.
        4. Take an hour-long break (too long).
    - **Optimized Routine** (if I could stick to it):
        1. Gather materials before starting.
        2. Study for 25 minutes with a timer.
        3. Take a short 5-minute break (instead of an hour).

3. Fill in the blanks:
- Keeping routines **simple** and **consistent** makes them easier to follow, but I feel like I just can't keep up.

Action Plan:
- I'll try using a timer to limit my break time, but I don't know if that will work because I always end up procrastinating.

Reflection:
- I realize that distractions are a big problem for me. I just need more discipline, but I'm not sure how to develop it.

3.3. Mission 3 Day 3: Maximizing Rewards for Habit Reinforcement

3.3.1. Theory:

Rewards play a crucial role in reinforcing habits. They help complete the habit loop and provide motivation to continue the behaviour. Effective rewards are:

1. **Personalized:** A reward should be meaningful to you. For one person, a reward might be a 10-minute break to enjoy a cup of tea; for another, it could be an episode of their favourite TV show.

2. **Immediate:** Especially in the early stages of habit formation, immediate rewards are powerful. If you have to wait too long to enjoy the fruits of your labour, you're less likely to maintain the behaviour.

3. **Aligned:** Rewards should align with your long-term goals. If your goal is to eat healthier, rewarding yourself with junk food would be counterproductive. Instead, choose a reward that supports your objective, such as buying a new workout outfit after sticking to a diet plan for a month.

Common Pitfalls to Avoid:

- **Negative Rewards:** These are rewards that undermine your progress, such as eating a sugary dessert after a workout.
- **Overemphasis on Rewards:** If the reward becomes more important than the habit itself, it can detract from the intrinsic motivation needed to sustain the habit in the long term.

Practical Exercise: Identify one habit you're trying to reinforce. List both the immediate and long-term rewards associated with it. Evaluate whether these rewards are effective and aligned with your goals.

Why it matters?

Mastering the use of rewards is essential for sustaining motivation and transforming good intentions into lasting behaviors.

Inspiring Thoughts to Reflect On

"Celebrate what you've accomplished, but raise the bar a little higher each time you succeed." – Mia Hamm.

3.3.2. Mission 3 Day 3 Worksheet:

Instruction: Think about the rewards you associate with your habits and how they motivate you.

Worksheet Sections:
1. **Current Rewards Analysis**
   For one habit you are working on, answer:
   - Habit: _____
   - Immediate Reward: _____
   - Long-term Reward: _____

2. **Personalization Exercise**
   Choose a habit you're trying to reinforce. What rewards could you add to make it more satisfying?
   - Habit: _____
   - Possible rewards:
     1. _____
     2. _____
     3. _____

3. **Fill in the Blanks**
   - Immediate rewards are effective because _____.
   - A long-term reward I would like is _____.

4. **Avoiding Pitfalls**
   List one reward that could negatively impact your progress and an alternative:

   Unhelpful rewards:

   _____

Alternatives:

3.3.3. Sample filled-up Worksheet for a Disciplined Person:

1. Why are rewards important in reinforcing habits?
- Rewards provide positive reinforcement, making it more likely for us to repeat the behaviour. Immediate rewards help in the early stages, while long-term rewards sustain the habit over time.

2. Exercise: Choose a habit and list a suitable immediate and long-term reward.
- **Habit:** Reading 20 pages every day.
    - **Immediate Reward:** A cup of tea after finishing the session.
    - **Long-term Reward:** Buying a new book at the end of the month.

3. Fill in the blanks:
- To be effective, rewards should be personalized and aligned with long-term goals.

Action Plan:
- I will switch my rewards for every mission to keep things fresh and interesting.

Reflection:

I've learned that the rewards don't need to be big. Simple pleasures like a warm drink are motivating enough.

3.3.4. Sample filled-up Worksheet for a Struggling Person:

1. Why are rewards important in reinforcing habits?
- Rewards are supposed to make you want to keep doing the habit, but I don't feel motivated by rewards. I end up rewarding myself too early, like before I've actually earned it.

2. Exercise: Choose a habit and list a suitable immediate and long-term reward.
- **Habit:** Finishing homework on time.
    - **Immediate Reward:** Watching YouTube videos (which I often do before finishing anyway).

    - **Long-term Reward:** Better grades (but this feels too far away to keep me motivated).

3. Fill in the blanks:

- Rewards should be **personalized**, but I just feel like I use them to procrastinate rather than push myself to finish tasks.

Action Plan:

- I guess I'll try not to reward myself until I actually finish my work, but I usually lose focus before that happens.

Reflection:

I think I'm using rewards the wrong way. It's hard to stay motivated when I give in too early.

For more resources, follow step-by-step:
- Scan the QR-code
- Register/Login Using Email-Id or Phone No.
- Browse through course videos
- Access Feeds for daily motivational & tricks for habit transformation

3.4. Mission 3 Day 4: Advanced Habit Tracking Techniques

3.4.1. Theory:

Habit tracking is more than just marking off a calendar—it's about gathering data to understand patterns and make improvements. Advanced tracking techniques can provide deeper insights into your habits:

1. **Digital Habit Trackers:** Apps that remind you of habits, provide data analytics, and help you identify patterns. For example, an app might show that you're more likely to skip a workout on mission ends, suggesting the need for a motivational boost on those days.

2. **Bullet Journals:** A more personalized and creative way of tracking habits, bullet journals allow you to log habits, reflect daily, and visually see your progress as a hands-on approach.

3. **Wearable Devices:** These devices are excellent for tracking physical habits such as steps, exercise, and sleep. They provide real-time feedback and can motivate you to stay active throughout the day.

Analyzing Habit Data: Once you have data from tracking, look for patterns. Identify what triggers cause you to skip habits and consider strategies to mitigate these. For example, if stress makes you skip workouts, introduce a calming pre-workout ritual.

Practical Exercise: Pick a habit you've been tracking. Analyze the data you've collected: what patterns emerge? What adjustments can you make based on this analysis to improve consistency?

Why it matters?

Advanced habit tracking goes beyond marking off days on a calendar—it provides deeper insights into your behavior. By leveraging tracking techniques, you identify patterns, measure progress, and spot areas for improvement. This proactive approach keeps you accountable and ensures your habits evolve with your needs. Advanced tracking methods help you maintain momentum by visualizing success, fostering motivation, and enabling data-driven adjustments.

Inspiring Thoughts to Reflect On

As Peter Drucker said – *"What gets measured gets improved."*

3.4.2. Mission 3 Day 4 Worksheet:

Instruction: This can help you learn how tracking can improve consistency and evaluate your current system.

Worksheet Sections:
1. **Tracking Method Review**
   What method do you currently use to track habits (if any)?

   o _____

Evaluate its effectiveness (1-10):

1. _____
2. _____
3. _____
4. _____
5. _____
6. _____
7. _____
8. _____
9. _____
10. _____

2. **Explore Tracking Tools**
   Which of these methods would you consider trying?

   o Digital Habit Tracker (App)

   o Bullet Journal

   o Wearable Device.

   Why?

   _____
   _____
   _____

3. **Fill in the Blanks**
    - "Tracking my habits helps me stay _____."
    - "I need to improve my tracking system by _____."

4. **Exercise: Habit Data Analysis**
   Pick one habit you've been tracking. Analyze your data:
    - Habit: _____
    - Pattern observed: _____
    - Next step to improve: _____

3.4.3. Sample filled-up Worksheet for a Disciplined Person:

Why is habit tracking important?
- Habit tracking helps maintain consistency, provides data for improvement, and holds me accountable.

2. Exercise: Track your water intake habit for the next 7 days and note any patterns.
- **Habit:** Drinking 8 glasses of water a day.
    - **Day 1:** 8 glasses
    - **Day 2:** 7 glasses
    - **Day 3:** 8 glasses
    - **Day 4:** 6 glasses
    - **Day 5:** 8 glasses
    - **Day 6:** 7 glasses
    - **Day 7:** 8 glasses
- **Pattern Observed:** On days when I'm busy, I tend to drink less water. Mission endings are also more challenging.

3. Fill in the blanks:
- Using **digital trackers** can remind me to complete my habits, while **journals** offer a more reflective approach.

Action Plan:
- I will set a timer on my phone to remind me to drink water every two hours.

Reflection:
- Tracking habits has made me more aware of my habits. Small changes can lead to significant improvements.

3.4.4. Sample filled-up Worksheet for a Struggling Person:

1. Why is habit tracking important?
- Habit tracking helps you stay accountable, but honestly, it feels like one more thing to do. When I fall behind, it just makes me feel bad about myself.

2. Exercise: Track your water intake habit for the next 7 days and note any patterns.
- **Habit:** Drinking 8 glasses of water.
    - **Day 1:** 3 glasses
    - **Day 2:** 4 glasses
    - **Day 3:** 2 glasses
    - **Day 4:** Forgot to track
    - **Day 5:** 3 glasses
    - **Day 6:** Forgot again
    - **Day 7:** 5 glasses
- **Pattern Observed:** I'm really inconsistent. Some days, I completely forget, and I'm not making any progress.

3. Fill in the blanks:
- Using **digital trackers** sounds easy, but I still forget. **Journals** might help, but I lose the motivation to write things down.

Action Plan:
- I'll set a reminder on my phone, but I don't know if that will help because I tend to ignore notifications when I'm busy.

Reflection:
- Tracking feels like a burden. When I fail to meet my goals, it just makes me feel worse about myself.

3.5. Mission 3 Day 5: Building Habit Streaks

3.5.1. Theory:

Building and maintaining habit streaks can create momentum and increase your motivation. A habit streak is the number of consecutive days you perform a habit without missing a day. The longer the streak, the more motivation you build to keep it going. The key components to building effective streaks are:

1. **Start Small:** Begin with a habit that is easy to maintain. For example, committing to 5 minutes of reading daily is more sustainable than aiming for an hour from the start.

2. **Visual Trackers:** Use calendars, habit-tracking apps, or even simple charts to keep your streaks visible. Seeing a growing streak can provide the motivation needed to continue.

3. **Consistency Over Perfection:** Understand that the goal is daily consistency. Missing a day is not a failure; it's an opportunity to restart with renewed focus.

Benefits of Habit Streaks:
- **Momentum Building:** Once you have a few days in a row, the desire not to break the streak becomes a powerful motivator.
- **Psychological Reward:** The feeling of accomplishment when seeing a long streak provides a psychological reward that reinforces the habit.

Practical Exercise: Identify a small habit to start building a streak. Create a visual tracker, such as a calendar or app, and commit to maintaining the habit daily for the next 21 days.

Key Takeaway: Habit streaks are powerful tools for building consistency. Focus on small, achievable steps, and use visual trackers to maintain motivation.

Why It Matters?

Habit streaks are powerful motivators that drive consistency and commitment. By maintaining a streak, you build momentum, making it easier to continue a behavior over time. Streaks create a sense of achievement and reinforce the belief that you are capable of lasting change. They transform small, daily actions into long-term success by linking progress to accountability. Building and sustaining streaks strengthens your dedication and turns good habits into an integral part of your life.

Inspiring Thoughts to Reflect On

"Don't break the chain. A little progress each day adds up to big results," says comedian Jerry Seinfeld, who emphasizes that daily effort builds momentum and mastery over time. Similarly, the phrase *"Momentum breeds motivation. Keep the streak alive"* reminds us of the power of consistency—small steps generate energy that fuels ongoing progress.

Robert Collier, a renowned self-improvement author, reinforces this with his words:

"Success is the sum of small efforts, repeated day in and day out," highlighting that lasting achievement is built through steady, committed actions. Together, these quotes reveal how consistency transforms small actions into meaningful success and growth.

For more resources, follow step-by-step:

- Scan the QR-code
- Register/Login Using Email-Id or Phone No.
- Browse through course videos
- Access Feeds for daily motivational & tricks for habit transformation

3.5.2. Mission 3 Day 5 Worksheet:

Instruction: Use this worksheet to focus on maintaining consistency by building streaks for habits.

Worksheet Sections:

1. **Current Streaks**
   What is your longest streak for any habit?
   - Habit: _____
   - Streak: _____

2. **Start Small**
   Choose one small habit you want to start building a streak for:
   - Habit: _____
   - How many consecutive days can you commit?

     _____ days

3. **Fill in the Blanks**
   - "A habit streak helps me stay motivated because _____."
   - "To maintain my streak, I will _____."

4. **Exercise: Streak Calendar**
   Create a mini calendar for the next 7 days and mark each day you successfully complete your chosen habit.

Day	Habit 1	Habit 2	Habit 3	Habit 4
Mon				
TUE				
WED				
THU				
FRI				
SAT				
SUN				

3.5.3. Sample filled-up Worksheet for a Disciplined Person:

1. What is a habit streak?
- A habit streak is the number of consecutive days you've completed a habit without missing a day.

2. Exercise: Set a streak goal for one of your habits and track your progress.
- **Habit:** Meditating daily.
  - **Goal:** Meditate for 10 minutes for the next 30 days.
  - **Current Streak:** 5 days in a row.

3. Fill in the blanks:
- Streaks build **momentum** and increase motivation to continue a habit.

Action Plan:
- I will use a visual tracker (a calendar) to mark my progress and motivate myself.

Reflection:
- Building a habit streak makes the idea of skipping a day feel like losing progress. It's a great way to keep myself accountable.

3.5.4. Sample filled-up Worksheet for a Struggling Person:

1. What is a habit streak?
- A habit streak is when you do something consistently without missing a day. I've never been able to build a long streak. I always miss a day and then give up.

2. Exercise: Set a streak goal for one of your habits and track your progress.
- **Habit:** Journaling every night.
  - **Goal:** Journal for 10 minutes every day for 7 days.
  - **Current Streak:** 2 days, then I missed a day.

3. Fill in the blanks:

- Streaks build **momentum**, but once I break the streak, I lose motivation to keep going.

Action Plan:

- I'll try not to beat myself up when I miss a day, but honestly, I feel like I fail more often than I succeed.

Reflection:

- I think I need to lower my expectations. Trying to build a streak feels overwhelming because I'm afraid of failing again.

For more resources, follow step-by-step:

- Scan the QR-code
- Register/Login Using Email-Id or Phone No.
- Browse through course videos
- Access Feeds for daily motivational & tricks for habit transformation

3.6. Mission 3 Day 6: Overcoming Streak Breaks

3.6.1. Theory:

Breaking a habit streak can feel like a major setback, but it's important to remember that it's a natural part of the habit-building process. Everyone encounters moments of inconsistency, and these breaks don't define your overall progress. What truly matters is how you respond and recover from them. Rather than seeing streak breaks as failures, view them as opportunities to learn and grow. Reflect on what caused the break, adjust your approach if necessary, and jump back into your routine. Rebuilding momentum quickly and forgiving yourself are key strategies for long-term success and sustainable habit formation. Here are some strategies:

1. **Acknowledge Without Self-Criticism:** Recognize the break without harsh judgment. Understand that it's normal for habits to falter occasionally.

2. **Analyze the Break:** Determine why the streak broke. Was it due to external factors (like an unexpected event) or internal ones (like a lack of motivation)? Understanding the reason helps in creating a better plan to avoid future breaks.

3. **Restart with Focus on Progress:** Instead of aiming for perfection, focus on getting back on track quickly. Start small again if needed and build up gradually.

Psychological Impact: The psychological impact of breaking a streak can lead to feelings of failure, disappointment, or frustration. However, it's crucial to reframe this experience as a valuable learning opportunity rather than a setback. Each break provides insight into the challenges or obstacles that disrupt your habits, helping you understand more about your triggers and patterns. By viewing streak breaks as moments of reflection rather than defeat, you can adjust your approach, strengthen your commitment, and build a more resilient habit system. Remember, long-term progress is not about perfection but about persistence and learning from each step.

Practical Exercise: Take some time to reflect on a habit streak you've recently broken. Write down the specific reasons or circumstances that led to the break—whether it was due to time constraints, lack of motivation, or external disruptions. Next, develop a clear plan to restart the habit and sustain it moving forward. Focus on practical changes you can implement, such as adjusting your routine, minimizing distractions, or setting reminders. Consider what steps you can take to prevent a similar break in the future, ensuring a more consistent and effective habit-building process.

Key Takeaway: Streak breaks are not failures but opportunities for growth. Acknowledge, analyze, and restart with a focus on resilience and progress.

Why It Matters?

Breaking a streak can feel discouraging, but it's a natural part of the growth process. Learning to recover quickly ensures that a minor setback doesn't turn into a major derailment. This skill builds resilience, teaching you to focus on progress rather than perfection. By understanding how to bounce back from streak breaks, you cultivate a growth mindset and maintain consistency in the long term. Overcoming breaks strengthens your commitment and proves that persistence is more important than perfection.

Inspiring Thoughts to Reflect On

"Fall seven times, stand up eight,"

It is a powerful Japanese proverb, reminding us of the resilience needed to persist through life's challenges. Similarly, the saying "Mistakes are proof you are trying. Progress comes from starting again" underscores that errors are part of the growth process, leading to progress each time we recommit. Another expression,

"Your journey isn't defined by a single step but by the determination to keep going."

It highlights that true success is shaped by unwavering perseverance. Together, these sayings emphasize that resilience, learning from setbacks, and consistent effort define our journey and progress forward.

3.6.2. Mission 3 Day 6 Worksheet:

Instruction: This worksheet guides you in learning how to recover and rebuild if you break your habit streak.

Worksheet Sections:

1. **Analyzing Streak Breaks**
   Think of a time when you broke a habit streak:
   - Habit: _____
   - Why did the streak break? _____

2. **Recovery Plan**
   Create a recovery plan for the next time you break a streak:
   - If I break my streak, I will:

1. _____
2. _____
3. _____

3. **Fill in the Blanks**
   - "When I break a streak, I tend to feel _____."
   - "I will focus on _____ to restart quickly."

4. **Exercise: Reflect & Restart**
   Write a reflection on one habit streak you broke recently. How will you restart and prevent future breaks?

   _____
   _____
   _____
   _____
   _____

3.6.3. Sample filled-up Worksheet for a Disciplined Person:

1. Why do streaks break?
- Streaks often break due to life interruptions, lack of motivation, or overwhelm from trying to do too much.

2. Exercise: Reflect on a time you broke a streak and analyze what went wrong.
- **Habit:** Working out daily.
    - **Reason for Break:** I missed three days because of a work trip.
    - **Analysis:** I didn't plan ahead or adjust my travel schedule. This led to a loss of momentum.

3. Fill in the blanks:
- Instead of self-criticism, I should focus on **rebuilding** and identifying the causes of streak breaks.

Action Plan: Next time I have a work trip, I'll create a simple workout routine I can do from my hotel room to keep the streak going.

Reflection:
- It's easy to be hard on myself when I break a streak, but it's important to focus on restarting rather than quitting.

3.6.4. Sample filled-up Worksheet for a Struggling Person:

. Why do streaks break?
- Streaks break when life gets in the way or when I'm too tired or stressed. Once I miss one day, it's hard to start again.

2. Exercise: Reflect on a time you broke a streak and analyze what went wrong.
- **Habit:** Reading every night before bed.
    - **Reason for Break:** I stayed up too late watching TV and was too tired to read.
    - **Analysis:** I let distractions take over and didn't prioritize my reading habits.

3. Fill in the blanks:

- Instead of self-criticism, I should focus on **rebuilding**, but I'm stuck in the cycle of feeling guilty and giving up.

Action Plan: I'll try reading earlier in the evening when I have more energy, but I'm not sure if that will work.

Reflection:

- It's really discouraging when I break a streak. I feel like once I fail, there's no point in trying again.

For more resources, follow step-by-step:

- Scan the QR-code
- Register/Login Using Email-Id or Phone No.
- Browse through course videos
- Access Feeds for daily motivational & tricks for habit transformation

3.7. Mission 3 Day 7: Mission 3 Reflection

3.7.1. Theory:

Reflecting on your progress and planning for future success is essential for continuous growth. Taking time to reflect allows you to identify what strategies and actions have been effective, as well as areas that need improvement. By understanding what's working and what isn't, you can make informed adjustments. Planning, on the other hand, sets a clear and actionable path forward, helping you stay focused on your goals. It ensures that your future efforts are aligned with your long-term vision, allowing you to build on your successes and address any challenges that arise along the way. Here's how to make the most out of this process:

1. **Reflect on Key Successes and Challenges:** Look back at your recent progress to identify which habits have been successfully established and which ones have faced difficulties. Consider the strategies that worked well for you and the circumstances that led to success. Equally important is to assess the challenges—what caused you to struggle or fall off track? Reflecting on both successes and challenges provides insight into what habits need to be reinforced and where adjustments can be made in your approach. This awareness will help you create a better, more sustainable plan moving forward.

2. **Identify Areas for Improvement:** Take a close look at the habits that require more attention and focus. Are there recurring obstacles that are preventing you from maintaining consistency? Whether it's distractions, time management issues, or lack of motivation, understanding these barriers is the first step toward overcoming them. Once you've identified the specific areas of weakness, you can begin planning targeted strategies to address them. This may involve making changes to your routine, finding new ways to stay accountable, or removing distractions that derail your progress.

3. **Set Specific, Measurable Goals:** For your upcoming habit-building efforts, set clear, specific, and measurable goals that are aligned with your overall objectives. These goals should be broken down into smaller, actionable steps to make them less overwhelming and more manageable. By doing this, you'll have a clear roadmap to follow and a sense of direction that will keep you focused. Measuring your

progress along the way allows you to celebrate small wins and course-correct when necessary, ensuring that you stay on track toward your long-term vision.

Practical Exercise: Create a Missionly habit plan. For your top three habits, list the cues, routines, and rewards that you will use. Reflect on what has worked well and where adjustments are needed.

Key Takeaway: Reflection is key to understanding your progress, and planning sets you up for future success. Use both tools to continuously refine your habits and achieve your goals.

Why It Matters?

Reflection turns experience into growth by helping you analyze your successes and challenges. By reviewing your progress, you gain clarity about what works and what doesn't, allowing you to refine your habits for greater success. Reflection fosters self-awareness and ensures that your actions remain aligned with your goals. It helps you celebrate achievements, address obstacles, and stay adaptable. Regular reflection transforms habit-building from a mechanical process into a meaningful journey of continuous improvement.

Inspiring Thoughts to Reflect On

"Life is a series of lessons which must be lived to be understood," said Ralph Waldo Emerson, highlighting that true wisdom emerges from lived experiences rather than theoretical knowledge. Similarly, the phrase "Take time to reflect on your journey. The insights gained will illuminate your path ahead." emphasizes the importance of pausing to consider the lessons learned, enabling us to make better decisions for the future. Together, these insights remind us that understanding and growth come from both experiencing life fully and reflecting on the journey, which enriches our path forward with clarity and purpose.

3.7.2. Mission 3 Day 7 Worksheet:

Instruction: Review your progress and plan for your ongoing habit journey.

Worksheet Sections:

1. **Reflection on Progress**
   Reflect on the past Mission. Which habit have you made the most progress with?
   - Habit: _____
   - Progress made: _____

2. **Planning Ahead**
   Write down one habit you want to focus on next Mission and the cues, routine, and rewards you will use:
   - Habit: _____
   - Cue: _____
   - Routine: _____
   - Reward: _____

3. **Fill in the Blanks**
   - "I feel most proud of _____ this Mission."
   - "Next Mission, I will focus on _____ to continue improving."

4. **Exercise: Missionly Habit Plan**
   Create a simple action plan for your top 3 habits for the next Mission. Include cues, routines, and rewards for each.

   _____
   _____
   _____
   _____
   _____
   _____
   _____
   _____

For more resources, follow step-by-step:

- Scan the QR-code
- Register/Login Using Email-Id or Phone No.
- Browse through course videos
- Access Feeds for daily motivational & tricks for habit transformation

3.7.3. Sample filled-up Worksheet for a Disciplined Person:

1. Reflection:
- **What have you learned about cues, routines, rewards, tracking, streaks, and streak breaks in this Mission?**
    - Cues are powerful triggers that initiate habits, routines must be simple and goal-oriented, rewards are key for motivation, and tracking helps maintain consistency. Streaks build momentum, but breaks happen. The important part is getting back on track without being overly critical of myself.

2. Exercise: Plan a new habit using all the strategies you've learned.
- **New Habit:** Journaling before bed.
    - **Cue:** Seeing my journal on my bedside table.
    - **Routine:** Writing for 10 minutes.
    - **Reward:** Reading for 15 minutes afterwards.
    - **Tracking:** Using a habit tracker app.
    - **Goal:** Maintain a 30-day streak.

3. Fill in the blanks:
- To succeed, I need to keep the routine **simple** and consistent and focus on **rewarding** myself daily.

Action Plan:
- I will start journaling tonight and use my tracking app to stay consistent.

Reflection:
- I feel more confident in my ability to form habits and maintain them using these advanced strategies. The key takeaway for me is the importance of self-awareness and adaptability in this process.

3.7.4. Sample filled-up Worksheet for a Struggling Person:

1. Reflection:

- **What have you learned about cues, routines, rewards, tracking, streaks, and streak breaks in this Mission?**
    - I've learned that I tend to sabotage my own progress. I set up cues and routines, but I get easily distracted. Tracking feels like a chore, and I break streaks all the time. Rewards don't seem to help, either. It feels like a constant battle to stay consistent.

2. Exercise: Plan a new habit using all the strategies you've learned.

- **New Habit:** Waking up 30 minutes earlier to study.
    - **Cue:** Setting an alarm.
    - **Routine:** Spend 15 minutes studying right after waking up.
    - **Reward:** Have a nice breakfast afterwards.
    - **Tracking:** Use a habit tracker app (though I've struggled with this).
    - **Goal:** Stick to it for 5 days this Mission.

3. Fill in the blanks:

- To succeed, I need to keep the routine **simple**, but I'm not sure if I can stick with it.

Action Plan:

- I'll try waking up earlier tomorrow, but I'm worried I'll hit the snooze button like I always do.

Reflection:

- I feel frustrated because I've tried to implement these strategies before, but I keep slipping up. I know what to do in theory, but putting it into practice is much harder than I thought.

Chapter – 4

4.1. Mission 4 Day 1: Habit Automation - Making Habits Stick with Minimal Effort

4.1.1. Theory:

Habit automation is about making behaviours so ingrained in your daily routine that they require minimal conscious effort. When you automate a habit, it becomes second nature, freeing up mental energy for other tasks. The key to habit automation is to start with a strong cue that naturally fits into your day, simplify the habit to make it easy, and reward yourself to reinforce the behaviour.

Steps to Automate Your Habit:

1. **Cue:** Identify a natural daily cue that will remind you to start the habit. The more consistent the cue, the easier it is to form the habit.
2. **Routine:** Establish a simple routine that follows the cue. This action should be straightforward and repeated daily.
3. **Reward:** Choose a reward that gives you immediate satisfaction, helping to reinforce the habit over time.
4. **Track Progress:** Consistent tracking allows you to monitor the habit's growth and see when it becomes automatic.

Example:

To automate the habit of drinking water in the morning, start by placing a glass of water on your bedside table the night before (cue).

This visual reminder will prompt you as soon as you wake up. The next step is to make it part of your morning routine by immediately drinking the water upon waking (routine).

By doing this consistently, you'll start to feel the immediate benefits of hydration, such as feeling more awake, energized, and refreshed (reward). Over time, this habit will become automatic, requiring little conscious effort to maintain.

Key Takeaway:

Automating habits reduces the mental load and helps them become effortless. Focus on using strong cues and consistent rewards to turn your desired behaviour into a natural part of your routine.

Why It Matters?

Habit automation simplifies your life by reducing the mental effort required for repetitive actions. When a habit becomes automatic, it integrates seamlessly into your routine, freeing up energy for more complex tasks. Automation ensures that positive behaviors continue even during busy or stressful times, providing stability and consistency. By making habits effortless, you create a system for sustainable growth and long-term success, allowing you to focus on higher-level goals without sacrificing progress.

Inspiring Thoughts to Reflect On

"First we make our habits, then our habits make us,"

It was observed by John Dryden, highlighting the powerful role habits play in shaping our lives and identities over time. Leonardo da Vinci adds a complementary insight with,

"Simplicity is the ultimate sophistication, even in the way we build our lives," suggesting that thoughtful, simple routines can lead to a refined and purposeful existence. Together, these reflections underscore the importance of building deliberate habits with a focus on simplicity, creating a foundation for a life that is both intentional and impactful.

4.1.2. Mission 4 Day 1 Worksheet:

Instruction: Today, you will begin automating one habit. Answer the questions, complete the exercises, and apply the actions.

Worksheet Sections:

1. What is Habit Automation?

- **Fill in the blank:**
  Habit automation is the process of making behaviours so routine they require _____.

2. Identify a Habit to Automate

- **Exercise:** Choose one habit you'd like to automate in your daily routine. Write it down:
    - Example: Drinking water in the morning.
    - **Your habit:**
    _____

3. Automating Your Habit

- **Fill in the blanks:**
  1. **Cue:** What natural daily cue will remind you to start the habit?
      - Example: Placing a glass of water by your bed.

      Your cue: _____

  2. **Routine:** What simple action will you perform when the cue happens?
      - Example: Drink water as soon as you wake up.

      Your routine: _____

  3. **Reward:** What reward will you give yourself?
      - Example: Feeling refreshed and hydrated.

      Your reward: _____

4. Start Tracking Your Habit

- **Exercise**: Create a simple tracking system to monitor your progress. How will you track your habits? (e.g., mark a calendar, use an app)
    - **Tracking method**:
    _____
    _____

5. Reflection:

- How did the first day of automating your habit go? Write reflecting on what worked and what didn't.

_____
_____
_____
_____
_____
_____
_____
_____

4.1.3. Sample filled-up Worksheet for a Disciplined Person:

1. **What is Habit Automation?**
   - Fill in the blank: Habit automation is the process of making behaviours so routine they require _____.
     - **Answer:** minimal conscious effort

2. **Identify a Habit of Automate**
   - Exercise: Choose one habit you'd like to automate in your daily routine. Write it down:
     - **Your habit:** Drinking water in the morning

3. **Automating Your Habit**
   - Fill in the blanks:

1. **Cue:** What natural daily cue will remind you to start the habit?
   - **Your cue:** Place a glass of water by your bed
2. **Routine:** What simple action will you perform when the cue happens?
   - **Your routine:** Drink the water as soon as you wake up
3. **Reward:** What reward will you give yourself?
   - **Your reward:** Feeling refreshed and hydrated
4. **Start Tracking Your Habit**
   - Exercise: Create a simple tracking system to monitor your progress. How will you track your habits? (e.g., mark a calendar, use an app)
     - **Tracking method:** Use a habit-tracking app
5. **Reflection:**
   - How did the first day of automating your habit go? Write 2-3 sentences reflecting on what worked and what didn't.

- **Reflection:** The habit automation went smoothly; having the glass of water ready by my bed was a good reminder. I felt more hydrated in the morning, which was motivating.

4.1.4. Sample filled-up Worksheet for a Struggling Person:

1. **What is Habit Automation?**
   - Fill in the blank: Habit automation is the process of making behaviours so routine they require _____.
     - **Answer:** minimal conscious effort

2. **Identify a Habit of Automate**
   - Exercise: Choose one habit you'd like to automate in your daily routine. Write it down:
     - **Your habit:** Brushing my teeth twice a day

3. **Automating Your Habit**
   - Fill in the blanks:

1. **Cue:** What natural daily cue will remind you to start the habit?
   - **Your cue:** Set a reminder on my phone

2. **Routine:** What simple action will you perform when the cue happens?
   - **Your routine:** Try to brush my teeth

3. **Reward:** What reward will you give yourself?
   - **Your reward:** No specific reward; just hoping it becomes a habit

4. **Start Tracking Your Habit**
   - Exercise: Create a simple tracking system to monitor your progress. How will you track your habits? (e.g., mark a calendar, use an app)
     - **Tracking method:** Use a checklist on my phone

5. **Reflection:**

- o How did the first day of automating your habit go? Write 2-3 sentences reflecting on what worked and what didn't.
    - **Reflection:** I forgot to set the reminder and missed brushing my teeth once. When I remembered, I felt frustrated for not sticking to the plan.

For more resources, follow step-by-step:

- ↓ Scan the QR-code
- ↓ Register/Login Using Email-Id or Phone No.
- ↓ Browse through course videos
- ↓ Access Feeds for daily motivational & tricks for habit transformation

4.2. Mission 4 Day 2: Reframing - Changing Your Perspective

4.2.1. Theory:

Reframing is the process of changing your perspective or mindset about a habit to make it more appealing and achievable. Often, people view habits they want to form as burdens or chores. Reframing involves looking at these habits from a different angle to see the benefits and positive aspects rather than the difficulties.

For example, if you find it challenging to start a morning exercise routine, try reframing it by focusing on the energizing effects and the sense of accomplishment it brings. Instead of saying, "I have to exercise," reframe it as "I get to boost my energy and mood for the day." This shift in perspective can alter how you feel about the habit, making it easier to adopt and maintain.

The act of reframing helps in aligning habits with your intrinsic motivations, making them feel less like obligations and more like opportunities for self-improvement. This change in mindset can also help overcome resistance and negative associations linked to certain habits.

Why It Matters?

Reframing is the art of seeing challenges and opportunities through a new lens. By shifting your perspective, you can transform negative thoughts into empowering ones, making difficult habits more manageable and rewarding. This mindset helps you stay motivated and resilient, especially when faced with setbacks. Reframing allows you to align your habits with a purpose, ensuring they feel meaningful and impactful. It's a powerful tool for personal growth and overcoming self-imposed limitations.

Inspiring Thoughts to Reflect On

"Change the way you look at things, and the things you look at change." – Wayne Dyer.

4.2.2. Mission 4 Day 2 Worksheet:

Instructions: Reframing is about shifting your mindset. Today, we'll practice turning negative habits into positive experiences.

Worksheet Sections:

1. What is Reframing?

- **Fill in the blank**:
  Reframing is changing the way you think about a _____.
  (Answer: situation or behaviour)

2. Identify a Habit to Reframe

- **Exercise**: Choose a habit you struggle with and reframe it.
    - **Old perspective**: I have to do this because _____.
    - **New perspective**: I get to do this because _____.

3. Create Positive Affirmations

- **Exercise**: Write down 2-3 positive affirmations about your habit.
    - Example: "I get to exercise to feel strong and energized."
    - **Your affirmations**:
        1. _____
        2. _____
        3. _____

4. Visualization

- **Exercise**: Take 5 minutes to visualize the positive outcomes of sticking to your habit. Write a brief description of what you imagined.

_____
_____
_____

4.2.3. Sample filled-up Worksheet for a Disciplined Person:

1. **What is Reframing?**
   - Fill in the blank: Reframing is changing the way you think about a _____.
     - **Answer:** situation or behaviour

2. **Identify a Habit to Reframe**
   - Exercise: Choose a habit you struggle with and reframe it.
     - **Old perspective:** I have to exercise because I need to lose weight.
     - **New perspective:** I get to exercise because it makes me feel strong and healthy.

3. **Create Positive Affirmations**
   - Exercise: Write down 2-3 positive affirmations about your habit.
     - **Affirmations:**
       1. "I get to exercise to feel strong and energized."
       2. "Exercise helps me stay healthy and improve my mood."
       3. "I am proud of the effort I put into my workouts."

4. **Visualization**
   - Exercise: Take 5 minutes to visualize the positive outcomes of sticking to your habit. Write a brief description of what you imagined.
     - **Visualization:** I imagined feeling more energetic and confident after exercising regularly. I saw myself enjoying outdoor activities and feeling proud of my progress.

4.2.4. Sample filled-up Worksheet for a Struggling Person:

1. **What is Reframing?**
    - Fill in the blank: Reframing is changing the way you think about a _____.
        - **Answer:** situation or behaviour

2. **Identify a Habit to Reframe**
    - Exercise: Choose a habit you struggle with and reframe it.
        - **Old perspective:** I have to study because it's required.
        - **New perspective:** I get to study because it helps me learn and grow.

3. **Create Positive Affirmations**
    - Exercise: Write down 2-3 positive affirmations about your habit.
        - **Affirmations:**
            1. "Studying helps me understand new things."
            2. "Learning is a step towards my goals."
            3. "I can improve my skills through study."

4. **Visualization**
    - Exercise: Take 5 minutes to visualize the positive outcomes of sticking to your habit. Write a brief description of what you imagined.
        - **Visualization:** I imagined feeling satisfied with my progress and understanding concepts better, but it was hard to stay focused on the positive outcome.

4.3. Mission 4 Day 3: Habit Chains - Linking Multiple Habits for Efficiency

4.3.1. Theory:

Habit chaining, also known as habit stacking, involves linking a new habit to an existing one to create a chain of actions. This technique leverages the power of existing habits to trigger new behaviours, making it easier to incorporate them into your daily routine. The process of habit chaining creates a sequence, where each habit serves as a cue for the next.

Start by identifying a habit you already perform consistently, such as having breakfast. Then, stack a new habit onto it, like reviewing your daily goals right after finishing breakfast. Over time, these linked actions form a chain, streamlining your routines and enhancing productivity.

How to Create Habit Chains:

- **Identify Existing Habits:** Start by listing habits you already perform daily, like brushing your teeth, making coffee, or checking emails. These become the anchors for adding new habits.

- **Add One Habit at a Time:** Attach a new habit to an existing one. For example, after brushing your teeth in the morning, you could immediately drink a glass of water. Once this habit is solidified, you can add another, like taking vitamins.

- **Use Clear Cues:** Ensure that the trigger for the new habit is clear and directly follows the existing habit. The cue acts as a signal for your brain to start the new behaviour.

- **Keep It Simple:** Avoid overloading the chain with too many new habits at once. Focus on consistency rather than complexity, gradually building the chain over time.

Advantages of Habit Chaining:

- Streamline your routine by grouping habits together.
- Enhances the likelihood of adopting new habits, as they piggyback on the success of existing ones.
- Reduces decision fatigue since one habit naturally triggers the next.

The beauty of habit chains lies in their efficiency and simplicity. By linking together related behaviors, you reduce the need for constant decision-making and conserve mental energy. When you engage in a sequence of actions—like brushing your teeth, followed by a short meditation, and then drinking water—you create a flow that feels natural and automatic over time. This chaining of habits helps you build momentum, as completing one action triggers the next. As you become more consistent, you can gradually add more positive habits into the chain, expanding it to enhance your productivity and well-being.

However, it's important to keep the chain manageable. Trying to incorporate too many new habits at once can lead to mental and physical fatigue, making it difficult to sustain long-term. Instead, focus on adding habits slowly, allowing each new behavior to become ingrained before introducing another. This steady, thoughtful approach helps prevent burnout and ensures that each habit has a lasting impact on your daily routine, leading to more sustainable success.

Why It Matters?

Habit chaining enhances efficiency by connecting new behaviors to existing routines. This approach leverages the power of association, making it easier to adopt positive changes. Habit chains create a natural flow in your day, reducing decision fatigue and strengthening consistency. By linking habits together, you build momentum, ensuring that progress becomes a seamless part of your lifestyle. This strategy is a practical and effective way to maximize productivity and establish long-lasting routines.

Inspiring Thoughts to Reflect On

"One habit sparks another, creating a ripple effect of growth."

It reminds us that positive habits often lead to more positive changes, compounding over time. This idea is echoed by Peter Drucker's insight on emphasizing the power of improving existing habits to foster growth and success.

"Efficiency is doing better what is already being done."

So, it is important to cultivate habits that build on each other, leading to greater efficiency and sustained personal development. By improving one habit, you set the stage for continuous growth and transformation in all areas of life.

4.3.2. Mission 4 Day 3 Worksheet:

Instructions: Today, we'll focus on building habit chains by linking one habit to another.

Worksheet Sections:

1. What is a Habit Chain?

- **Fill in the blank**:

Habit chains involve _____ multiple habits together in a sequence. (Answer: linking)

2. Create Your Habit Chain

- **Exercise**: Choose a routine and create a habit chain.

Example:
- **Anchor habit**: Brushing your teeth.
- **Habit 1**: Drink water.
- **Habit 2**: Meditate for 5 minutes.

Your habit chain:

Anchor habit: _____

    Habit 1: _____

    Habit 2: _____

    Habit 3: _____

    Habit 4: _____

Note (*if any*):

3. Plan Your Routine

- **Exercise**: When will you start your habit chain? Write down the time of day and where it will happen.

Time	Place

4. Reflection:

- How did your habit chain flow today? Did linking habits make them easier? Write 2-3 sentences.

_____

_____

_____

_____

_____

4.3.3. Sample filled-up Worksheet for a Disciplined Person:

1. **What is a Habit Chain?**
   - Fill in the blank: Habit chains involve _____ multiple habits together in a sequence.
     - **Answer:** linking

2. **Create Your Habit Chain**
   - Exercise: Choose a routine and create a habit chain.
     - **Your habit chain:**
       - **Anchor habit:** Brushing your teeth
       - **Habit 1:** Drink water
       - **Habit 2:** Meditate for 5 minutes
       - **Habit 3 (optional):** Stretch for 2 minutes

3. **Plan Your Routine**
   - Exercise: When will you start your habit chain? Write down the time of day and where it will happen.
     - **Time:** 7:00 AM
     - **Place:** Bathroom

4. **Reflection:**
   - How did your habit chain flow today? Did linking habits make them easier? Write 2-3 sentences.
     - **Reflection:** Linking the habits together made the routine feel more natural. Starting with brushing my teeth set a positive tone for the other activities, and the chain felt efficient.

4.3.4. Sample filled-up Worksheet for a Struggling Person:

1. **What is a Habit Chain?**

    o Fill in the blank: Habit chains involve _____ multiple habits together in a sequence.

    - **Answer:** linking

2. **Create Your Habit Chain**

    o Exercise: Choose a routine and create a habit chain.

    - **Your habit chain:**
        - **Anchor habit:** Making my bed
        - **Habit 1:** Check emails
        - **Habit 2:** Eat breakfast
        - **Habit 3 (optional):** Read a book

3. **Plan Your Routine**

    o Exercise: When will you start your habit chain? Write down the time of day and where it will happen.

    - **Time:** 8:00 AM
    - **Place:** Bedroom

4. **Reflection:**

    o How did your habit chain flow today? Did linking habits make them easier? Write 2-3 sentences.

    - **Reflection:** I struggled to link all the habits together. I got distracted and missed some steps in the chain, which made the routine feel overwhelming.

4.4. Mission 4 Day 4: Environmental Design - Shaping Your Space for Habit Success

4.4.1. Theory

Environmental design is the practice of organizing your physical space to support positive habits and minimize distractions. By altering your environment, you can make good habits more convenient and bad habits harder to perform. This method leverages the fact that our surroundings have a significant impact on our behaviour.

Strategies for Environmental Design:

- **Create Convenience:** Place items that promote good habits within easy reach. For example, keep healthy snacks at the front of the fridge to encourage healthy eating or place your workout clothes next to your bed to prompt morning exercise.

- **Remove Triggers for Bad Habits:** Make it difficult to engage in unwanted habits by removing or hiding cues. If you're trying to cut down on screen time, place your phone in another room during meals or study sessions.

- **Designate Habit Zones:** Allocate specific areas for different activities. For example, designate a corner of your room for reading, free of distractions. This helps your brain associate certain environments with specific habits, reinforcing the behaviour.

- **Use Visual Reminders:** Add visual prompts in your environment to reinforce habits. Sticky notes, reminders, or motivational posters can serve as cues that nudge you toward your desired actions.

Benefits of Environmental Design:

- Reduces reliance on willpower by making habits easier or harder to perform, depending on your goal.
- Promotes consistency by aligning your surroundings with your habits.
- Helps in building lasting habits by associating specific environments with certain behaviours.

Why It Matters?

Basically, environmental design plays a crucial role in shaping our habits by strategically organizing our surroundings to promote positive behavior and minimize distractions. By making good habits more accessible and bad habits less convenient, this approach reduces reliance on willpower and increases consistency. Whether it's placing workout gear by your bed to encourage morning exercise or designating specific areas for focused activities, environmental design aligns your space with your goals. This technique not only helps build lasting habits but also reinforces them by associating specific environments with desired behaviors, making it easier to maintain a productive and intentional lifestyle.

Inspiring Thoughts to Reflect On

"Your environment will eat your willpower for breakfast,"

as James Clear wisely states, underscores the powerful influence our surroundings have on our behavior and habits. This idea aligns with the notion that, as the unknown author suggests,

"Design the life you want by shaping the spaces you live in."

When we intentionally create an environment that supports our goals, it becomes easier to form positive habits and avoid distractions. By shaping our surroundings to align with our desired outcomes, we effectively reduce the need for willpower, making it easier to achieve long-term success and fulfillment.

4.4.2. Mission 4 Day 4 Worksheet:

Instructions: Your environment can influence your habits. Today, you will design a space that supports your habits.

Worksheet Sections:

1. What is Environmental Design?

- **Fill in the blank**:

    Environmental design is shaping your _____ to support your habits. (Answer: space)

2. Design Your Space

- **Exercise**: Choose one habit you want to improve and design your environment around it.

    - **Example:** To improve focus, create a distraction-free workspace.
    - **Your habit:** _____
    - **Your environment design**:
      _____

3. Environmental Cues

- **Exercise**: What visual or physical cues will you add to your space to reinforce your habit?

    - For example, place a sticky note reminder or put workout clothes on a chair.
    - **Your cues**: _____

4. Reflection:

- How did changing your environment affect your habits today?

    _____
    _____
    _____

4.4.3. Sample filled-up Worksheet for a Disciplined Person:
1. **What is Environmental Design?**
   - Fill in the blank: Environmental design is shaping your **space** to support your habits.

2. **Design Your Space**
   - Exercise: Choose one habit you want to improve and design your environment around it.
     - **Your habit:** Improving focus
     - **Your environment design:** Create a clutter-free workspace with a comfortable chair and a clear desk.

3. **Environmental Cues**
   - Exercise: What visual or physical cues will you add to your space to reinforce your habit?
     - **Your cues:** Place a motivational quote on the wall and keep study materials organized on the desk.

4. **Reflection:**
   - How did changing your environment affect your habits today? Write 2-3 sentences.
     - **Reflection:** The organized study space helped me concentrate better. The motivational quote was a good reminder to stay focused on my tasks.

4.4.4. Sample filled-up Worksheet for a Struggling Person:
1. **What is Environmental Design?**
   - Fill in the blank: Environmental design is shaping your _____ to support your habits.
     - **Answer:** space

2. **Design Your Space**
   - Exercise: Choose one habit you want to improve and design your environment around it.

- **Your habit:** Exercising at home
- **Your environment design:** I tried to set up a space, but it's still cluttered, and I haven't made much progress.

3. **Environmental Cues**
    - Exercise: What visual or physical cues will you add to your space to reinforce your habit?
        - **Your cues:** I put a workout schedule on the wall, but it's not very noticeable.

4. **Reflection:**
    - How did changing your environment affect your habits today? Write 2-3 sentences.

Reflection: Changing the environment didn't help much. I still found excuses not to exercise and felt like the setup wasn't motivating enough.

For more resources, follow step-by-step:
- Scan the QR-code
- Register/Login Using Email-Id or Phone No.
- Browse through course videos
- Access Feeds for daily motivational & tricks for habit transformation

4.5. Mission 4 Day 5: Behavioural Substitution - Replacing Negative Habits with Positive Ones

4.5.1. Theory

Behavioural substitution involves replacing a negative habit with a more positive alternative. This technique works by addressing the underlying cue and reward of the original habit while swapping out the behaviour itself. By substituting the habit, you create a pathway to more beneficial behaviours without relying solely on willpower.

Steps to Implement Behavioural Substitution:

- **Identify the Cue:** Determine what triggers the negative habit. For instance, stress might prompt snacking on unhealthy foods. Understanding the cue is key to finding an appropriate substitute.

- **Choose a Positive Substitute:** Select a new habit that satisfies the same cue and reward. For example, if stress leads to snacking, substitute it with deep breathing exercises or drinking a cup of herbal tea.

- **Prepare Your Environment:** Make the positive substitute accessible. If you're replacing unhealthy snacks, keep fruits or nuts within easy reach, and remove junk food from sight.

- **Practice Consistency:** Repetition is crucial for substitution to take root. Each time the cue arises, consciously choose the new behaviour until it becomes the default response.

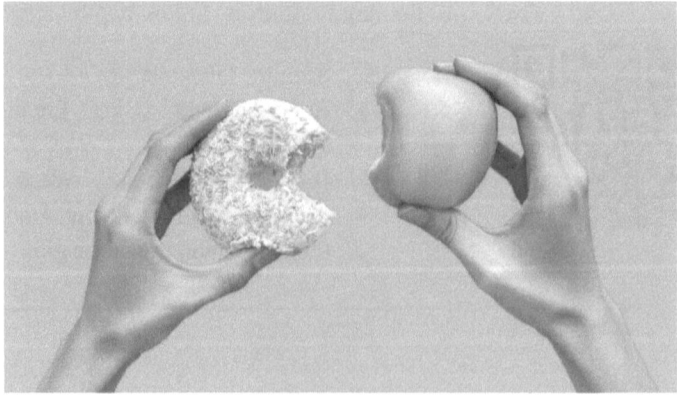

Advantages of Behavioural Substitution:
- Reduces the likelihood of reverting to old, negative habits by providing an alternative.
- Reinforce positive behaviours that align with your goals.
- Empowers you to take control of habit change without feeling deprived.

Why It Matters?

So, behavioral substitution is a highly effective strategy for transforming negative habits into positive ones. By understanding the triggers and rewards of your habits, you can consciously replace harmful behaviors with healthier alternatives, leading to lasting change. This method reduces reliance on willpower and creates a sustainable framework for habit transformation. With consistency and thoughtful preparation, behavioral substitution empowers you to take control of your actions, reinforcing behaviors that align with your personal and long-term goals. It offers a practical, empowering approach to building better habits and living a more intentional life.

Inspiring Thoughts to Reflect On

"What we achieve, we sustain through systems, not sporadic effort."

The quote above highlights the importance of creating reliable systems for success rather than relying on inconsistent bursts of energy or motivation. So, one needs to acknowledge even minor achievements, which can provide the motivation to continue. Together, these quotes convey that lasting success is built on sustainable systems, and even small progress is worth celebrating as it fuels ongoing momentum toward greater achievements.

"Celebrate progress, no matter how small, and you'll keep moving forward."

4.5.2. Mission 4 Day 5 Worksheet:

Instructions: Replace a negative habit with a positive one. Identify cues and rewards to help with the transition.

Worksheet Sections:

1. What is Behavioural Substitution?

- **Fill in the blank**:

    Behavioural substitution is replacing a _____ habit with a _____ one. (Answer: negative, positive)

2. Identify a Negative Habit

- **Exercise**: Choose a negative habit you want to replace.
    - Example: Snacking on junk food when stressed.
    - **Your negative habits**: _____

    _____

    _____

    _____

3. Substitute with a Positive Habit

- **Exercise**: Find a positive habit to substitute. Use the same cue and reward as the negative habit.
    - **Cue**: _____
    - **New habit**: _____
    - **Reward**: _____

4. Practice Your Substitution

- **Exercise**: Each time you feel the cue for the negative habit, practice your new habit instead.

5. Reflection:

- Did you successfully substitute your negative habit today? What was challenging? Write 2-3 sentences.

_____

_____

_____

_____

4.5.3. Sample filled-up Worksheet for a Disciplined Person:

1. **What is Behavioural Substitution?**
    - Fill in the blank: Behavioural substitution is replacing a _____ habit with a _____ one.
        - **Answer:** negative, positive

2. **Identify a Negative Habit**
    - Exercise: Choose a negative habit you want to replace.
        - **Your negative habit:** Snacking on junk food when stressed

3. **Substitute with a Positive Habit**
    - Exercise: Find a positive habit to substitute. Use the same cue and reward as the negative habit.
        - **Cue:** Feeling stressed
        - **New habit:** Eating a piece of fruit or drinking herbal tea
        - **Reward:** Feeling healthier and less guilty

4. **Practice Your Substitution**
    - Exercise: Each time you feel the cue for the negative habit, practice your new habit instead.

5. **Reflection:**
    - Did you successfully substitute your negative habit today? What was challenging? Write 2-3 sentences.
        - **Reflection:** I managed to substitute junk food with healthier options, but it was challenging to overcome the immediate craving. The fruit and tea helped, and I felt better afterwards.

4.5.4. Sample filled-up Worksheet for a Struggling Person:

1. **What is Behavioural Substitution?**
   - Fill in the blank: Behavioural substitution is replacing a _____ habit with a _____ one.
     - **Answer:** negative, positive

2. **Identify a Negative Habit**
   - Exercise: Choose a negative habit you want to replace.
     - **Your negative habit:** Procrastinating on projects.

3. **Substitute with a Positive Habit**
   - Exercise: Find a positive habit to substitute. Use the same cue and reward as the negative habit.
     - **Cue:** Feeling overwhelmed by deadlines
     - **New habit:** Break projects into smaller tasks and work on them
     - **Reward:** Sense of accomplishment and less stress

4. **Practice Your Substitution**
   - Exercise:

   Each time I feel the cue for the negative habit, I chose to practice the new habit instead.

5. **Reflection:**
   - Did you successfully substitute your negative habit today? What was challenging? Write 2-3 sentences.
     - **Reflection:** I tried to break tasks into smaller steps, but I still procrastinated. It was hard to stay on track and manage time effectively.

4.6. Mission 4 Day 6: Reinforcement Systems - Sustaining Long-Term Habits

4.6.1. Theory

Reinforcement systems are methods used to maintain and strengthen habits over the long term. Positive reinforcement encourages repetition by rewarding the desired behaviour. By strategically using reinforcement, you can build a support system that keeps you motivated and on track with your habits.

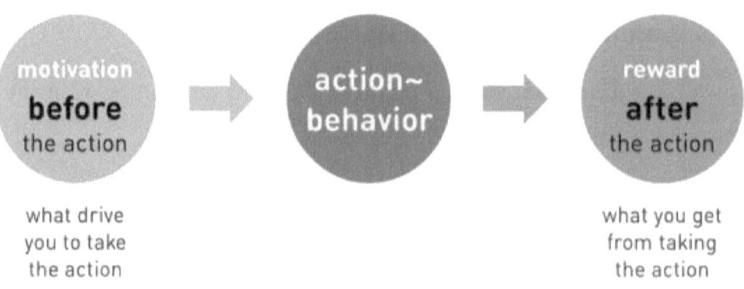

Types of Reinforcement Systems:

- **Immediate Rewards:** Provide small rewards immediately after completing a habit. This could be a piece of dark chocolate after finishing a workout or a relaxing bath after a productive day. Immediate rewards help create a positive association with the habit.

- **Delayed Rewards:** Set up larger rewards for long-term consistency. For instance, treat yourself to a new gadget after maintaining a habit streak for a month. Delayed rewards build anticipation and motivate sustained effort.

- **Accountability Partners:** Use social reinforcement by involving friends or family. Share your progress, set up regular check-ins, or establish a friendly competition. Accountability boosts motivation and provides encouragement when needed.

- **Self-Acknowledgement:** Reflect on your progress and celebrate milestones. Acknowledge your efforts, even if the habit isn't yet perfect. Positive self-talk reinforces the belief that you can succeed.

Why It Matters?

So, reinforcement systems play a vital role in cultivating and sustaining habits over time. By employing immediate and delayed rewards, you create positive associations that encourage consistent behavior. Accountability partners enhance motivation by providing support and fostering a sense of community, while self-acknowledgment reinforces your progress and boosts your confidence. Together, these methods form a comprehensive approach to habit maintenance, ensuring that your efforts lead to long-lasting change. By strategically implementing reinforcement systems, you empower yourself to stay committed to your goals, ultimately paving the way for a more fulfilling and productive life.

Inspiring Thoughts to Reflect On

Consistent efforts, supported by reinforcement systems like rewards and accountability, lead to lasting success and transformation. Walt Disney was a visionary entrepreneur, animator, and film producer who co-founded The Walt Disney Company. His creative genius and leadership reshaped entertainment, focusing on the power of action, commitment, and persistence to achieve long-term success. He quoted –

> *"The way to get started is to quit talking and begin doing."*

For more resources, follow step-by-step:
- Scan the QR-code
- Register/Login Using Email-Id or Phone No.
- Browse through course videos
- Access Feeds for daily motivational & tricks for habit transformation

4.6.2. Mission 4 Day 6 Worksheet:

Instructions: Explore different reinforcement systems to maintain your habits over time. Design a personalized plan using immediate and delayed rewards and reflect on how these strategies will support your long-term success.

Worksheet Sections:

1. Understanding Reinforcement Systems

Definition:
Reinforcement systems use rewards and positive feedback to sustain habits. They help maintain motivation and consistency over the long term.

Instructions:
Read the definition and answer the following questions.

Questions:

1. **What are reinforcement systems, and why are they important for sustaining habits?**

   _____

   _____

2. **List and briefly describe the four types of reinforcement.**
   - Immediate Reinforcement:

     _____

   - Delayed Reinforcement:

     _____

   - Intrinsic Reinforcement:

     _____

   - Extrinsic Reinforcement:

     _____

2. Designing Your Reinforcement System

Principles:

- Identify what motivates you and tailor your reinforcement accordingly.
- Use a combination of intrinsic and extrinsic rewards for balance.
- Set up a system of milestones and rewards to track progress.
- Adjust your reinforcement system as your habits evolve.

Instructions:
Design a reinforcement system for a habit you are working on. Follow the steps below.

Exercise:

1. **Identify Your Habit:**
    - _____

2. **Define Your Motivations:**
    - Intrinsic Motivation:
      _____

    - Extrinsic Motivation:
      _____

3. **Set Up Milestones:**
    - Short-Term Milestones:
      _____

    - Long-Term Milestones:
      _____

4. **Plan Your Rewards:**
    - Immediate Reward:
      _____

- Delayed Reward:

    _____

5. **Track Your Progress:**

   How will you monitor your progress and adjust your reinforcement system?

   _____
   _____
   _____

3. Reflection

Instructions:

Reflect on the following and write your responses.

1. **How will combining different types of reinforcement impact your habit formation?**

   _____
   _____
   _____

2. **Describe any adjustments you might need to make to your reinforcement system.**

   _____
   _____
   _____

4.6.3. Sample filled-up Worksheet for a Disciplined Person:

1. **Understanding Reinforcement Systems**

Definition: Reinforcement systems use rewards and positive feedback to sustain habits. They help maintain motivation and consistency over the long term.

Questions:

- What are reinforcement systems, and why are they important for sustaining habits?

Answer: Reinforcement systems are strategies that use rewards and positive feedback to encourage habit persistence. They are important because they help maintain motivation and consistency, making it easier to sustain habits over time.

- List and briefly describe the four types of reinforcement.
  1. **Immediate Reinforcement:** Reward received shortly after the behaviour (e.g., enjoying a treat right after a workout).
  2. **Delayed Reinforcement:** Reward received after a period of time (e.g., saving money for a big purchase).
  3. **Intrinsic Reinforcement:** Internal satisfaction or pleasure from the behaviour itself (e.g., feeling proud of personal progress).
  4. **Extrinsic Reinforcement:** External rewards or recognition (e.g., receiving praise or a certificate).

2. **Designing Your Reinforcement System**
   - **Exercise:**
     1. **Identify Your Habit:**
        - **Habit:** Exercising regularly
     2. **Define Your Motivations:**
        - **Intrinsic Motivation:** Enjoyment from feeling fit and healthy
        - **Extrinsic Motivation:** Compliments from others and achieving fitness goals

3. **Set Up Milestones:**
    - **Short-Term Milestones:** Completing a Mission of workouts
    - **Long-Term Milestones:** Achieving a personal fitness goal, such as running a certain distance.
4. **Plan Your Rewards:**
    - **Immediate Reward:** Enjoying a relaxing bath after each workout
    - **Delayed Reward:** Treating myself to a new workout outfit after reaching a long-term milestone
5. **Track Your Progress:**
    - **Tracking method:** Use a fitness app to log workouts and monitor progress. Adjust the reinforcement system based on progress and motivation levels.

3. **Reflection**
    - **Questions:**
        1. How will combining different types of reinforcement impact your habit formation?
            - **Answer:** Combining different types of reinforcement will provide both immediate and long-term motivation, making it easier to stay committed to the habit and increasing overall satisfaction.
        2. Describe any adjustments you might need to make to your reinforcement system.
            - **Answer:** I might need to adjust the rewards based on how well they motivate me or add more variety to keep the reinforcement system engaging.

4.6.4. Sample filled-up Worksheet for a Struggling Person:

1. **Understanding Reinforcement Systems**
   - **Definition:** Reinforcement systems use rewards and positive feedback to sustain habits. They help maintain motivation and consistency over the long term.
   - **Questions:**
     1. What are reinforcement systems, and why are they important for sustaining habits?
        - **Answer:** Reinforcement systems use rewards to keep you motivated, but I find it hard to stick to a system consistently.
     2. List and briefly describe the four types of reinforcement.
        - **Immediate Reinforcement:** Rewards given right away
        - **Delayed Reinforcement:** Rewards given later on
        - **Intrinsic Reinforcement:** Feeling good about the behaviour
        - **Extrinsic Reinforcement:** External rewards like praise

2. **Designing Your Reinforcement System**
   - **Exercise:**
     1. **Identify Your Habit:**
        - **Habit:** Exercising regularly
     2. **Define Your Motivations:**
        - **Intrinsic Motivation:** Wanting to feel healthier
        - **Extrinsic Motivation:** Aiming for visible fitness results

3. **Set Up Milestones:**
    - **Short-Term Milestones:** Working out twice a Mission
    - **Long-Term Milestones:** Achieving a fitness goal
4. **Plan Your Rewards:**
    - **Immediate Reward:** Watching a TV show after a workout
    - **Delayed Reward:** Buying new workout clothes
5. **Track Your Progress:**
    - **Tracking method:** Trying to use a fitness app but struggling to update it regularly

3. **Reflection**
    - **Questions:**
        1. How will combining different types of reinforcement impact your habit formation?
            - **Answer:** Combining reinforcements might help, but I find it challenging to stay consistent with rewards.
        2. Describe any adjustments you might need to make to your reinforcement system.
            - **Answer:** I need to make rewards more immediate and adjust the system to fit my daily routine better.

4.7. Mission 4 Day 7: Review and Reflect - Mission 4 Wrap-Up

4.7.1. Theory

Reflection and celebration are essential practices for consolidating your habit transformation journey. Reflection allows you to assess what strategies worked, identify areas of improvement, and set new goals. Celebrating achievements, no matter how small reinforces the positive behaviours you've been building and boosts motivation for future growth. This day is about taking a step back to appreciate your progress and planning how to continue moving forward.

Steps for Effective Reflection:

- **Review Your Progress:** Take some time to go over your habit-tracking data, journals, or any notes you've made throughout the Mission. Assess which habits you've successfully implemented and which ones still need work. Look for patterns or triggers that influenced your habits positively or negatively.

- **Identify Challenges:** Reflect on the obstacles you encountered. Were there specific times when maintaining a habit was particularly difficult? Understanding these challenges can help you develop strategies to overcome them in the future.

- **Acknowledge Growth:** Celebrate the small wins and milestones. Reflect on how even minor changes have contributed to your overall growth. Acknowledging progress fosters a positive mindset and motivates you to keep moving forward.

- **Set New Goals:** Based on your reflections, decide on the next steps. Set clear, actionable goals for the upcoming Mission. Make adjustments to your habit strategies if necessary, and continue building on the foundation you've established.

Benefits of Reflection and Celebration:

- **Reinforces Positive Habits:** By celebrating your achievements, you create a reward system that encourages continued effort.

- **Enhances Self-Awareness:** Reflection helps you understand your behaviours, motivations, and triggers, providing valuable insights for further habit transformation.

- **Builds Resilience:** Acknowledging both successes and challenges builds mental resilience, empowering you to handle setbacks and continue your progress.

Why It Matters?

Therefore, reflection and celebration are pivotal components of your habit transformation journey. By regularly assessing your progress, identifying challenges, and acknowledging growth, you create a strong foundation for continuous improvement. Celebrating even the smallest achievements reinforces positive behaviors and fuels motivation for future endeavors. This practice not only enhances self-awareness, offering insights into your habits and triggers, but also builds resilience, equipping you to face obstacles with confidence. Ultimately, by incorporating reflection and celebration into your routine, you ensure that your journey toward lasting change remains purposeful and fulfilling, paving the way for ongoing success.

Inspiring Thoughts to Reflect On

Baltasar Gracián, a 17th-century Spanish philosopher and Jesuit priest, emphasized that wisdom is born through introspection. His writings on ethics and personal conduct suggest that self-awareness is essential for growth and navigating life's challenges. He said –

> *"Self-reflection is the school of wisdom."*

So, pause and remember—what you don't reflect on, you can't improve. Through reflection, we transform experience into knowledge and intention into action.

4.7.2. Mission 4 Day 7 Worksheet:

Instructions: Review the key techniques from Mission 4 and assess their impact on your habit formation. Reflect on your progress, address any challenges, and create a plan to continue applying these strategies effectively.

1.7.5. Worksheet Sections:

1. Mission 4 Recap

Instructions:
Review the key concepts covered during Mission 4 and answer the questions below.

Questions:

1. **List the topics covered in Mission 4.**

   _____
   _____
   _____
   _____
   _____
   _____

2. **What advanced techniques have you successfully integrated into your habit formation?**

   _____
   _____

3. **Describe any challenges you encountered during Mission 4 and how you addressed them.**

   _____
   _____
   _____

2. Reflecting on Your Progress

Instructions:
Answer the following reflection questions.

1. **How have the advanced techniques impacted your overall habit formation?**

    _____

    _____

    _____

2. **What improvements have you noticed in your habit consistency and effectiveness?**

    _____

    _____

3. Personal Action Plan

Instructions:
Create an action plan for continuing to apply the techniques learned in Mission 4.

Action Plan:

1. **What techniques will you continue to use and why?**

    _____

    _____

2. **How will you maintain and reinforce these habits moving forward?**

    _____

    _____

3. **Set specific goals for the next month related to your habit formation.**
    - Goal 1:
      _____
    - Goal 2:
      _____
    - Goal 3:
      _____

4. Feedback
Instructions:
Provide any feedback or thoughts on the Mission 4 sessions.

1. **What did you find most useful about Mission 4?**

   _____
   _____
   _____
   _____

2. **What could be improved or added for future sessions?**

   _____
   _____
   _____
   _____

4.7.3. Sample filled-up Worksheet for a Disciplined Person:

1. **Mission 4 Recap**

    Q. List the topics covered in Mission 4.

    1. Habit Automation
    2. Reframing
    3. Habit Chains
    4. Environmental Design
    5. Behavioural Substitution
    6. Reinforcement Systems

    Q. What advanced techniques have you successfully integrated into your habit formation?

    Answer: Habit automation and reinforcement systems were particularly effective in sustaining my habits. Habit chains also helped in making my routines more efficient.

    Q. Describe any challenges you encountered during Mission 4 and how you addressed them.

    Answer: One challenge was maintaining consistency with new habits. I addressed it by setting up clear cues and rewards and adjusting my environment to better support my routines.

2. **Reflecting on Your Progress**

    Q. How have the advanced techniques impacted your overall habit formation?

    Answer: The advanced techniques have significantly improved my habit formation by providing structure and motivation. I feel more confident in maintaining and evolving my habits.

    Q. What improvements have you noticed in your habit consistency and effectiveness?

    Answer: I've noticed increased consistency in my routines and greater effectiveness in forming new habits. The reinforcement systems and habit chains have been particularly helpful.

3. **Personal Action Plan**

   Q. What techniques will you continue to use and why?

   Answer: I will continue using habit automation and reinforcement systems because they effectively support habit formation and motivation.

   Q. How will you maintain and reinforce these habits moving forward?

   Answer: I will regularly review my progress and adjust my reinforcement system as needed. I'll also continue using cues and rewards to stay motivated.

   Set specific goals for the next month related to your habit formation.

   - **Goal 1:** Establish a new habit chain for morning and evening routines.
   - **Goal 2:** Implement an additional reinforcement system for a new habit.
   - **Goal 3:** Improve consistency in tracking and reflecting on habit progress.

4. **Feedback**

   o **Questions:**

   Q. What did you find most useful about Mission 4?

   o **Answer:** The reinforcement systems and environmental design strategies were particularly useful in sustaining long-term habits.

   Q. What could be improved or added for future sessions?

   o **Answer:** It would be helpful to include more examples and interactive activities to practice applying the techniques.

4.7.4. Sample filled-up Worksheet for a Struggling Person:

1. **Mission 4 Recap**

    Q. List the topics covered in Mission 4.

    - Habit Automation
    - Reframing
    - Habit Chains
    - Environmental Design
    - Behavioural Substitution
    - Reinforcement Systems

    Q. What advanced techniques have you successfully integrated into your habit formation?

    Answer: I've struggled to fully integrate the techniques but have made some progress with habit automation and reinforcement systems.

    Q. Describe any challenges you encountered during Mission 4 and how you addressed them.

    Answer: I had difficulty staying consistent with new habits and reinforcement strategies. I tried adjusting reminders and rewards but still faced challenges.

2. **Reflecting on Your Progress**

    Q. How have the advanced techniques impacted your overall habit formation?

    Answer: The techniques helped a bit, but I find it hard to apply them consistently in my routine.

    Q. What improvements have you noticed in your habit consistency and effectiveness?

    Answer: I'm still working on improving consistency. Some habits have become slightly more regular, but I need more time and practice.

3. **Personal Action Plan**

   Q. What techniques will you continue to use and why?

   Answer: I will continue using habit automation and try to implement reinforcement systems better.

   Q. How will you maintain and reinforce these habits moving forward?

   Answer: I'll need to make reminders more noticeable and find a better way to track progress.

   Q. Set specific goals for the next month related to your habit formation.

   Goal 1: Improve consistency in daily habits

   Goal 2: Better implementation of reinforcement strategies

   Goal 3: Develop a more effective tracking system

4. **Feedback**

   Q. What did you find most useful about Mission 4?

   Answer: The ideas for designing the environment and reinforcement systems were useful but hard to apply.

   Q. What could be improved or added for future sessions?

   Answer: More practical examples and additional support for applying techniques would be helpful.

Chapter – 5

5.1. Mission 5 Day 1: Understanding Your Unique Habit Profile

5.1.1. Theory:

Understanding your unique habit profile is the key to forming lasting habits that suit your lifestyle. Everyone has different motivations, challenges, and tendencies when it comes to habits, so discovering your own profile is essential to success.

A habit profile is essentially a personalized assessment of your behaviours and tendencies. It shows what drives your habits and what holds you back. Knowing these details allows you to tailor your strategies for habit formation. For example, some people are motivated by rewards, while others need strong routines or environmental cues to stay on track.

Your habit profile is made up of several components. First is **motivation**, What inspires you to start and stick with a habit? It could be the energy boost from morning exercise or the satisfaction of completing a task. Then, there's **resistance**: the obstacles that make it harder to maintain habits. Recognizing these resistances helps in finding ways to overcome them.

Another crucial part is **cues and triggers**. These are environmental or emotional signals that prompt your habits. For instance, the sound of your alarm might trigger your morning routine, or feeling stressed might lead to unhealthy snacking. Identifying these cues helps you become more aware of what sets your habits in motion. Lastly, consider the **rewards**: What do you gain from the habit? It could be the endorphin rush after a workout or the sense of accomplishment from a completed task.

To understand your habit profile better, try tracking your habits over a Mission. Look for patterns: which habits are you consistent with, and which ones fluctuate? Analyze what triggers your successful habits and what disrupts them. For example, if your goal is morning exercise, note what motivates you (energy boost), what resists it (morning tiredness), the cue (alarm clock), and the reward (endorphin rush).

Here are **five highlights** of your unique **habit profile**:

- Personalized Assessment
- Components of Habit Profile
- Motivation and Resistance
- Cues and Triggers
- Tracking and Analysis

Why It Matters?

Every individual has a unique pattern of habits influenced by their personality, lifestyle, and environment. By understanding your unique habit profile, you gain insight into what motivates you, what challenges you, and what strategies work best for you. This self-awareness allows you to tailor your habit-building process, ensuring that it aligns with your strengths and addresses your weaknesses. Personalizing your approach not only improves your chances of success but also makes the journey more fulfilling and sustainable.

Inspiring Thoughts to Reflect On

Sun Tzu, an ancient Chinese military strategist, is best known for his work The Art of War. His wisdom emphasizes the importance of self-awareness and understanding one's strengths and weaknesses to achieve success, whether in battle or life. He quoted –

> "*Know yourself, and you will win all battles.*"

Therefore, individuals should try to align their actions with their aspirations. "*Your habits are as unique as your fingerprint—shape them to fit your goals.*"

5.1.2. Mission 5 Day 1 Worksheet:

Objective: Analyze and understand your unique habit profile to personalize habit formation strategies.

Instructions:

1. **Track Your Habits:** Use the table below to record your habits for the next 5 days.
2. **Identify Triggers and Rewards:** After each habit, write down what triggered the action and what reward or feeling you received after.
3. **Analyze Your Habits:** At the end of 5 days, reflect on the patterns, motivations, and resistances.

Habit	Motivation (Why?)	Trigger (What prompts it?)	Reward (What's the outcome?)

Questions to Answer:

1. What habits were easy for you to maintain? Why do you think that is?

   _____
   _____
   _____
   _____

2. Which habits were hard to keep up with? What made them difficult?

   _____
   _____
   _____

3. Were there any surprising triggers or rewards that you hadn't noticed before?

   _____
   _____
   _____
   _____
   _____

5.1.3. Sample filled-up Worksheet for a Disciplined Person:

Objective: Analyze and understand your unique habit profile to personalize habit formation strategies.

Instructions:

1. **Track Your Habits:** Use the table below to record your habits for the next 5 days.
2. **Identify Triggers and Rewards:** After each habit, write down what triggered the action and what reward or feeling you received after.
3. **Analyze Your Habits:** At the end of 5 days, reflect on the patterns, motivations, and resistances.

Habit	Motivation (Why?)	Trigger (What prompts it?)	Reward (What's the outcome?)
Wake up at 5 AM	To start the day productively	Alarm clock	Feel energized and ahead of schedule
Study for 2 hours	To stay on top of my academics	Scheduled time block	Satisfaction with completing the study session
Exercise for 30 min	To stay fit and healthy	Post-study break	Endorphin boost and improved focus
Journal daily	To reflect and maintain mental clarity	Before bedtime routine	Mental relaxation and self-awareness
Avoid phone until 9 AM.	To improve morning focus	Morning distraction	Increased concentration and calmness

Questions to Answer:

1. **What habits were easy for you to maintain? Why do you think that is?**

   o Waking up at 5 AM and exercising were easier to maintain. I have set a clear structure for my mornings, and the sense of accomplishment drives me to continue.

2. **Which habits were hard to keep up with? What made them difficult?**

   o Avoiding the phone until 9 AM was harder. The urge to check notifications is strong, especially when there's downtime after waking up.

3. **Were there any surprising triggers or rewards that you hadn't noticed before?**

   o I noticed that starting my day productively (waking up early and exercising) keeps me motivated to study longer. The satisfaction from being ahead of schedule was greater than I expected.

5.1.4. Sample filled-up Worksheet for a Struggling Person:

Objective: Analyze and understand your unique habit profile to personalize habit formation strategies.

Instructions:

1. **Track Your Habits:** Use the table below to record your habits for the next 5 days.

2. **Identify Triggers and Rewards:** After each habit, write down what triggered the action and what reward or feeling you received after.

3. **Analyze Your Habits:** At the end of 5 days, reflect on the patterns, motivations, and resistances.

Habit	Motivation (Why?)	Trigger (What prompts it?)	Reward (What's the outcome?)
Waking up at 6:30 AM	To get more time for morning tasks	Alarm clock	Extra time, but often feel tired
Study for 1 hour	To keep up with assignments	Due dates, guilt for procrastination	Relief, but stress about not doing enough
Exercise for 15 min	To stay active and healthy	Seeing workout gear in the room	Sense of accomplishment, but often tired
Avoid social media in the morning.	To stay focused on tasks	The habit of checking notifications	Disappointment when I fail
Journal for 5 minutes	To reflect and reduce stress	Bedtime, feeling overwhelmed	Small mental relief, but sometimes skipped

Questions to Answer:

1. **What habits were easy for you to maintain? Why do you think that is?**

    o Journaling and brief exercises were somewhat easier to maintain, but only when I was already in the mood for it. These habits provide small moments of relief, but I often struggle with consistency.

2. **Which habits were hard to keep up with? What made them difficult?**

    o Avoiding social media and waking up on time was the hardest. I struggle with energy levels in the morning, and the habit of checking my phone is deeply ingrained.

3. **Were there any surprising triggers or rewards that you hadn't noticed before?**

    o   I didn't realize how much guilt from procrastination triggers my study habits and how checking notifications in the morning immediately derails my focus.

For more resources, follow step-by-step:

- Scan the QR-code
- Register/Login Using Email-Id or Phone No.
- Browse through course videos
- Access Feeds for daily motivational & tricks for habit transformation

5.2. Mission 5 Day 2: Tailoring Habit Techniques to Your Personality

5.2.1. Theory:

Tailoring habit techniques to fit your personality is a crucial step in building lasting habits. This approach recognizes that not all strategies work the same for everyone. By customizing habits to suit who you are, you can increase your motivation, enhance consistency, and improve the overall effectiveness of habit formation.

Why is personalization so important? Simply put, when habits align with your natural tendencies, they become easier to maintain. For example, an extroverted person might thrive in a group workout setting, while an introvert might find solitary activities like journaling or meditation more rewarding. Tailoring your strategies helps you find methods that not only work but feel right for you.

Understanding your personality is the first step in this process. Ask yourself a few questions: Are you more introverted or extroverted? Do you prefer structure in your routines, or do you like flexibility? Are you driven by internal motivations, like personal growth, or external rewards, like praise from others? How do you handle challenges: by pushing through obstacles alone or by seeking support from others? These insights give you a roadmap for choosing the right habit techniques.

Matching techniques to personality involves applying these insights to your daily routines. For instance, introverts might benefit from quiet, reflective habits like meditation or solo workouts. They can create a calming environment and set a specific time each day for their habits. Extroverts, on the other hand, might find success with social habits, like joining group exercise classes or pairing up with an accountability partner. Structured personalities thrive with detailed routines and step-by-step plans, while flexible personalities do better with a spontaneous approach, allowing room for adjustments as needed.

A practical example is an introvert aiming to meditate daily. By setting a consistent time and creating a peaceful environment, they align the habit with their need for quiet reflection. The reward—internal peace and clarity—fits their personality, making the habit easier to sustain.

So, the key points of tailoring habit techniques to fit personality are:

- **Importance of Personalization:**
Customizing habit strategies to match individual personalities enhances motivation, consistency, and effectiveness in habit formation.

- **Personality Insights:** Understanding whether you are introverted or extroverted, and whether you prefer structure or flexibility, provides a roadmap for selecting suitable habit techniques.

- **Aligning Habits with Natural Tendencies:** When habits reflect personal tendencies, they become easier to maintain, increasing the likelihood of long-term success.

- **Matching Techniques to Personality Types:** Introverts may thrive with reflective practices, while extroverts might benefit from social habits, ensuring the methods resonate with their preferences.

- **Practical Application:** Setting consistent times and creating environments that support your personality, like a calming space for meditation, makes habits easier to sustain and enhances overall satisfaction.

Why It Matters?

Leveraging your strengths and addressing your weaknesses ensures a balanced and effective approach to habit-building. Your strengths are assets that propel you forward, while your weaknesses are opportunities for growth. By recognizing and using both, you create a plan that plays to your advantages while mitigating obstacles. This strategy builds confidence and resilience, enabling you to overcome challenges and achieve your goals with greater efficiency and clarity.

Inspiring Thoughts to Reflect On

Ralph Waldo Emerson, a renowned American essayist and philosopher, often explored the relationship between adversity and growth. He said –

"Our strength grows out of our weaknesses."

5.2.2. Mission 5 Day 2 Worksheet:

Objective: *Align habit strategies to your personality traits.*

Instructions:

1. **Personality Reflection:** *Answer the following questions to identify key aspects of your personality:*
   - Are you more introverted or extroverted?

   _____

   - Do you prefer structured routines or flexible schedules?

   _____

   - Are you motivated more by internal factors (personal goals) or external ones (recognition, rewards)?

   _____

2. **Fill in the Blank:**
   - I am more of a(n) _____ (introvert/extrovert).
   - My preference for routines is _____ (structured/flexible).
   - I am motivated more by _____ (internal/external) factors.

3. **Match Strategies:** Based on your answers, suggest habit techniques that align with your traits. For example:
   - Introverts may prefer habits like journaling or reading.
   - Extroverts may benefit from social accountability, like working out with a friend.

   _____

   _____

_____

_____

Questions to Answer:

1. How do you think your personality affects your ability to form habits?

   _____

   _____

   _____

2. Which strategies do you think would work best for you based on your traits?

   _____

   _____

   _____

5.2.3. Sample filled-up Worksheet for a Disciplined Person:

1. **Personality Reflection:**
    - **Are you more introverted or extroverted?** Introverted.
    - **Do you prefer structured routines or flexible schedules?** Structured routines.
    - **Are you motivated more by internal factors (personal goals) or external ones (recognition, rewards)?** Internal factors.

2. **Fill in the Blank:**
    - I am more of an **introvert**.
    - My preference for routines is **structured**.
    - I am motivated more by **internal** factors.

Match Strategies:

- Since I am introverted and prefer structured routines, habits like journaling and solo study sessions fit well. To enhance motivation, I should track progress and set personal goals rather than rely on external rewards.

Questions to Answer:

1. **How do you think your personality affects your ability to form habits?**
    - My introverted nature makes me more comfortable with individual tasks like reading and journaling. I find it easier to stick to habits that involve self-reflection and quiet time.

2. **Which strategies do you think would work best for you based on your traits?**
    - Structured schedules, self-reflection through journaling, and tracking progress without external validation would be most effective.

5.2.4. Sample filled-up Worksheet for a Struggling Person:

1. **Personality Reflection:**

   o **Are you more introverted or extroverted?** Introverted.

   o **Do you prefer structured routines or flexible schedules?** Flexible schedules.

   o **Are you motivated more by internal factors (personal goals) or external ones (recognition, rewards)?** External factors (due dates, reminders from others).

2. **Fill in the Blank:**

   o I am more of an **introvert**.

   o My preference for routines is **flexible**.

   o I am motivated more by **external** factors.

Match Strategies:

- As an introvert, I prefer activities like journaling, reading, or solo study sessions, but I need external accountability for motivation. A strategy like working with a study buddy or setting specific deadlines might help me stick to habits.

Questions to Answer:

1. **How do you think your personality affects your ability to form habits?**

   o My introverted nature means I avoid group activities that might keep me more accountable. My preference for flexibility sometimes results in me letting things slide without structure.

2. **Which strategies do you think would work best for you based on your traits?**

   o Flexible schedules combined with external reminders (apps, deadlines) and perhaps some social accountability (like sharing progress with a friend) would be the best fit.

5.3. Mission 5 Day 3: Building a Personalized Habit Toolkit

5.3.1. Theory:

Building a personalized habit toolkit is like assembling a toolbox tailored specifically for your journey toward habit success. Just as a toolkit for a craftsman contains different tools for different jobs, your habit toolkit is filled with strategies and resources that help you form, track, and maintain your habits effectively.

What is a habit toolkit? It's a collection of methods and resources customized to fit your unique needs. This toolkit includes various tools designed to support your progress and increase your chances of long-term success. It could contain a mix of physical, digital, or mental strategies to keep you on track and motivated.

Essential tools for your habit toolkit might include a habit tracker, which allows you to monitor and analyze your progress. Visualizing your consistency over time can be a powerful motivator. Reminders and alarms are simple but effective tools that nudge you to take action.

If you're someone who benefits from social support, accountability partners can provide the motivation and encouragement you need. Rewards play a crucial role in reinforcing positive behaviours, whether they are small treats or moments of relaxation. Lastly, reflection journals help you document your journey, offering insights into what works and what doesn't.

Customizing your toolkit is key to making it work for you. Select tools that align with your personality, preferences, and goals. For example, if you enjoy technology, digital tools like apps and smartwatches may suit you best. Alternatively, if you prefer a more hands-on approach, using a physical journal or a wall calendar can be effective. As your habits and goals evolve, so should your toolkit. Regularly review and update it to ensure you have the right mix of strategies to keep you moving forward.

A practical example could be someone aiming to improve their physical health. Their toolkit might include a fitness tracker to monitor workouts, daily reminders to stay active, a support group for accountability, a journal for tracking meals, and a reward system for reaching fitness milestones.

In short, **a personalized habit toolkit** gives you the right tools to build and sustain your habits. By including a variety of tools tailored to your specific goals, you create a system that adapts and grows with you, ensuring your path to success.

Why It Matters?

A customized habit plan allows you to take control of your growth journey by designing habits that suit your needs, goals, and circumstances. Personalizing your plan increases the likelihood of consistency and success. It empowers you to align your actions with your long-term vision while adapting to life's changes. A well-thought-out plan ensures that your efforts are both focused and flexible, giving you the tools to thrive regardless of external challenges.

Inspiring Thoughts to Reflect On

Antoine de Saint-Exupéry, the celebrated French writer and aviator, highlights the essential role of planning in achieving our aspirations. Known for works like The Little Prince, Saint-Exupéry believed that structured action transforms dreams into reality. He said –

"A goal without a plan is just a wish."

For more resources, follow step-by-step:

- Scan the QR-code
- Register/Login Using Email-Id or Phone No.
- Browse through course videos
- Access Feeds for daily motivational & tricks for habit transformation

5.3.2. Mission 5 Day 3 Worksheet:

Objective: *Create a toolkit of resources to support your habit formation.*

Instructions:

1. **Toolkit Components:** *Use the space below to list tools you'll include in your habit toolkit.*
    - **Reminder Systems:** What reminders will you use? (e.g., phone alarms, sticky notes)
    - **Habit Trackers:** How will you track your progress? (e.g., apps, journals)
    - **Rewards:** What rewards will motivate you to stay consistent?

Toolkit Component	Type (Digital/Physical)	Purpose (Why are you using it?)

Questions to Answer:

1. Which tools do you think will be most effective for you? Why?

___

___

___

___

2. How will you keep your toolkit updated as your habits evolve?

___

___

___

___

5.3.3. Sample filled-up Worksheet for a Disciplined Person:

Objective: Create a toolkit of resources to support your habit formation.

Toolkit Component	Type (Digital/Physical)	Purpose (Why are you using it?)
Phone alarms	Digital	To ensure I wake up and stay on schedule
Habit tracker app	Digital	To track progress and maintain streaks
Physical journal	Physical	To reflect on daily habits and clear mental clutter
Rewards list	Physical	To provide self-rewards for consistent habit formation

Questions to Answer:

1. **Which tools do you think will be most effective for you? Why?**

   The habit tracker app and phone alarms are the most effective because they provide consistent reminders and visual proof of progress, which motivates me.

2. **How will you keep your toolkit updated as your habits evolve?**

   I will regularly review my habits, remove or adjust reminders that are no longer needed, and add new tools or rewards as I progress.

5.3.4. Sample filled-up Worksheet for a Struggling Person:

Objective: *Create a toolkit of resources to support your habit formation.*

Toolkit Component	Type (Digital/Physical)	Purpose (Why are you using it?)
Phone alarms	Digital	To remind me of tasks like studying or journaling
Habit tracker app	Digital	To monitor my progress and show streaks
Sticky notes	Physical	To remind myself of key habits throughout the day
Rewards list	Physical	To motivate myself with small treats or breaks for success

Questions to Answer:

1. **Which tools do you think will be most effective for you? Why?**

    Sticky notes and phone alarms will be effective because they offer quick, visible reminders. The habit tracker app might motivate me if I can keep a streak going.

2. **How will you keep your toolkit updated as your habits evolve?**

    I will adjust my reminders and rewards, adding new ones as I succeed or removing tasks that become too overwhelming.

5.4. Mission 5 Day 4: Overcoming Personal Challenges in Habit Formation

5.4.1. Theory:

Overcoming personal challenges in habit formation is an essential step toward lasting success. Each person faces unique obstacles on their journey to building new habits, but understanding these challenges is the first move in conquering them. Let's explore some common issues people encounter and strategies to address them.

Common Personal Challenges include:

- **Lack of Time:** Life can get hectic, and finding room for new habits can feel impossible.

- **Low Motivation:** It's natural for motivation to fluctuate. The initial excitement of starting a new habit often fades, making it hard to maintain the drive.

- **Emotional Resistance:** Change can be intimidating, and feelings of anxiety or fear may create internal barriers.

- **Inconsistent Environment:** An unstable or ever-changing environment can disrupt routines and make it difficult to stick to new habits.

These obstacles are normal, and everyone experiences them at some point. The key lies in identifying your specific challenges and addressing them with targeted strategies.

Effective Strategies to Overcome Challenges:

- **Time Management:** Break habits into smaller, more manageable chunks. If you struggle to find time for exercise, for example, try starting with just five minutes a day. Gradually increase the time as you get more comfortable.

- **Motivation Boosters:** Use reminders to keep the habit fresh in your mind, set rewards to celebrate small wins, and involve an accountability partner for support. These techniques help sustain interest and make the process more enjoyable.

- **Emotional Support:** If emotional resistance is holding you back, seek help from a coach, mentor, or support group. Talking through your fears can make them feel less daunting.
- **Environmental Adjustments:** Design your surroundings to support your habit. Keep distractions away and create a dedicated space for your activity, whether it's a study nook, a meditation corner, or a workout area.

A Practical Example might involve a learner struggling with low motivation to study daily. To overcome this, they could set small, achievable goals like studying for just 15 minutes, using a study buddy for support, and rewarding themselves after each session.

Why It Matters?

Overcoming personal challenges in habit formation is crucial because these obstacles can halt progress and diminish motivation. Recognizing and addressing issues like lack of time, low motivation, emotional resistance, and an inconsistent environment allows individuals to build resilience and adapt habits to fit their unique circumstances. When people identify and tackle these challenges, they build a stronger foundation for lasting change, transforming daily actions into sustained routines that lead to long-term success. This process not only reinforces commitment but also empowers individuals to achieve their goals, making habit formation an accessible and rewarding journey for anyone.

Inspiring Thoughts to Reflect On

Winston Churchill. Known for his steadfast leadership during World War II, Churchill's words remind us that persistence is essential, especially when overcoming personal obstacles. He said –

"Success is not final; failure is not fatal: It is the courage to continue that counts."

Overcoming challenges in habit formation often requires resilience and courage, just as Churchill urged, highlighting that persistence is vital.

5.4.2. Mission 5 Day 4 Worksheet:

Objective: *Identify challenges and develop strategies to overcome them.*

Instructions:

1. **Identify Your Challenges:** *Fill in the table below with your personal habit formation challenges.*

Challenge	Example	Strategy to Overcome
Sample: Lack of Time	Not enough time to work out	Break it into 10-minute chunks
Lack of Time		
Low Motivation		
Inconsistent Routine		

2. **Reflection:**

   Q. What has been the hardest part of building new habits?

   _____
   _____
   _____
   _____
   _____
   _____

Q. How can you use the strategies you've identified to overcome these challenges?

_____

_____

_____

_____

Questions to Answer:

Q. What are the top two challenges you face when trying to build habits?

_____

_____

_____

_____

Q. How will you apply the strategies you identified to tackle these challenges?

_____

_____

_____

_____

_____

5.4.3. Sample filled-up Worksheet for a Disciplined Person:

Objective: Identify challenges and develop strategies to overcome them.

Instructions:

Identify Your Challenges: Fill in the table below with your personal habit formation challenges.

Challenge	Example	Strategy to Overcome
Lack of Time	Not enough time for long workouts	Break workout into shorter, manageable 15-minute slots
Low Motivation	Feeling tired after studying	Use a quick 5-minute break or short walk to re-energize
Inconsistent Routine	Difficulty sticking to meal times	Plan and prepare meals in advance for consistency

Reflection:
1. **What has been the hardest part of building new habits?**
    - Sticking to a consistent routine when my energy dips, especially after long study sessions, has been the hardest.
2. **How can you use the strategies you've identified to overcome these challenges?**
    - By scheduling shorter, manageable chunks of time for difficult habits and using small breaks to refresh myself, I can overcome dips in motivation and avoid burnout.

Questions to Answer:
1. **What are the top two challenges you face when trying to build habits?**
    - Low motivation after studying and inconsistent routines with eating and workouts.
2. **How will you apply the strategies you identified to tackle these challenges?**

- I will incorporate small breaks after studying to refresh my energy and plan meals/workouts in advance to avoid inconsistency.

5.4.4. Sample filled-up Worksheet for a Struggling Person:

Objective: Identify challenges and develop strategies to overcome them.

Instructions:

Identify Your Challenges: Fill in the table below with your personal habit formation challenges.

Challenge	Example	Strategy to Overcome
Lack of Time	Not enough time to study	Set smaller study goals (e.g., 20 minutes per session)
Low Motivation	Difficulty starting tasks	Use the "5-minute rule" to just begin the task
Inconsistent Routine	Trouble maintaining a regular routine	Create more flexible time slots for habits (e.g., morning/afternoon study options)

Reflection:

1. **What has been the hardest part of building new habits?**
   - The hardest part has been low motivation and a lack of energy. I often feel overwhelmed by larger goals and end up procrastinating.

2. **How can you use the strategies you've identified to overcome these challenges?**
   - By breaking tasks into smaller, more manageable pieces, I can reduce the feeling of being overwhelmed. I also plan to start tasks for just 5 minutes to overcome initial resistance.

Questions to Answer:

1. **What are the top two challenges you face when trying to build habits?**

    o   Low motivation and inconsistent routines due to fluctuating energy levels and workload.

2. **How will you apply the strategies you identified to tackle these challenges?**

    o   I will set smaller goals (e.g., study for just 20 minutes) and schedule tasks at different times of the day when I feel more capable of handling them.

For more resources, follow step-by-step:

- Scan the QR-code
- Register/Login Using Email-Id or Phone No.
- Browse through course videos
- Access Feeds for daily motivational & tricks for habit transformation

5.5. Mission 5 Day 5: Leveraging Strengths and Addressing Weaknesses

5.5.1. Theory:

Leveraging Strengths and Addressing Weaknesses is a crucial part of building successful habits. Self-awareness allows you to harness your natural abilities and work on areas that might be holding you back. By understanding your strengths and weaknesses, you can tailor your habit strategies to suit your unique personality, making the journey easier and more rewarding.

The Power of Self-Awareness: Self-awareness is like having a map for your personal growth. When you know your strengths, you can use them to make habit formation more enjoyable and manageable. On the other hand, being aware of your weaknesses helps you anticipate challenges and find ways to overcome them. This dual approach—leveraging strengths while addressing weaknesses—removes many barriers to success.

Identifying Your Strengths: Start by reflecting on habits or behaviours that come naturally to you. What tasks do you find easy or enjoyable? For example, if you have a knack for organization, you can use that skill to plan and schedule your new habits. Strengths are your built-in tools, and using them can provide a strong foundation for developing new routines.

Addressing Your Weaknesses: Weaknesses are those areas where you frequently encounter setbacks. Maybe you struggle with procrastination or get easily distracted by social media. Identifying these habits that often derail your progress is the first step to addressing them. To mitigate weaknesses, think of strategies that can help—like using focus apps to limit phone use or breaking tasks into smaller, manageable parts.

A Practical Example: Imagine you have strong organizational skills but get easily distracted by social media. To leverage your organizational strength, you could meticulously plan your habits with detailed schedules. To address the distraction, set time limits on phone use and employ focus apps to keep you on track.

Why It Matters?

Understanding and leveraging your strengths accelerates your growth by amplifying what already works for you. At the same time, addressing weaknesses helps you overcome the obstacles that hinder progress. This dual approach ensures a holistic method for habit-building, balancing self-improvement with self-acceptance. By focusing on strengths, you gain confidence and momentum; by tackling weaknesses, you grow more resilient and adaptable. This balance is the foundation for lasting personal development.

Inspiring Thoughts to Reflect On

There is a saying that goes like this –

"Strengths give you the leverage to lift yourself higher; weaknesses teach you how to grow."

It captures the essence of personal development by emphasizing self-awareness as a path to empowerment. Similarly, it also reminds us that embracing our strengths, while learning from obstacles, is a key to enduring success. Therefore, always remember that –

"The most successful people focus on their strengths but never shy away from challenges."

For more resources, follow step-by-step:
- Scan the QR-code
- Register/Login Using Email-Id or Phone No.
- Browse through course videos
- Access Feeds for daily motivational & tricks for habit transformation

5.5.2. Mission 5 Day 5 Worksheet:

Objective: Use self-awareness to build on your strengths and improve on weaknesses.

Instructions:
1. **Strengths and Weaknesses Exercise:**
    - **Strengths:** Write down three things you are good at (e.g., organizing and keeping a schedule).
    - **Weaknesses:** Write down three habits you struggle with (e.g., procrastination, lack of focus).

Strength	How it helps with habits	Weakness	How it hinders habits

2. **Action Plan:** For each strength, think of a way to use it to support your habits. For each weakness, write one strategy to address it.

Strength	Action Plan	Weakness	Action Plan

Questions to Answer:

1. How can you use your strengths to make habit-building easier?

   _____

   _____

   _____

2. What one step will you take to improve on a weakness?

   _____

   _____

   _____

5.5.3. Sample filled-up Worksheet for a Disciplined Person:

Strength	How it helps with habits	Weakness	How it hinders habits
Good time management	Helps me stay consistent with routines	Procrastination	Delays tasks, breaking habit momentum
Self-discipline	Sticking to an early wake-up routine	Lack of energy	This leads to skipping workouts or studying
Organization	Makes it easier to plan tasks and habits	Overthinking	Causes stress and reduces focus

Action Plan:

Strength	Action Plan	Weakness	Action Plan
Good time management	Set clear goals and time blocks daily	Procrastination	Break tasks into smaller, manageable goals
Self-discipline	Continue using alarms to stay consistent	Lack of energy	Take small breaks to recover and re-energize

Questions to Answer:

1. **How can you use your strengths to make habit-building easier?**
    - I can use my time management and organization skills to set clear goals and plan tasks, ensuring I stay on track.

2. **What one step will you take to improve on a weakness?**
    - I will break tasks into smaller chunks to avoid procrastination and include short breaks to prevent fatigue.

5.5.4. Sample filled-up Worksheet for a Struggling Person:

Strength	How it helps with habits	Weakness	How it hinders habits
Good listener	Helps with learning from others' advice	Procrastination	I delay important tasks
Adaptability	Can adjust when routines don't work	Low energy levels	I often feel too tired to do tasks
Empathy	Supports working well with others	Easily distracted	I lose focus when studying or working

Action Plan:

Strength	Action Plan	Weakness	Action Plan
Good listener	Seek advice and accountability from friends	Procrastination	Break down tasks into smaller steps
Adaptability	Experiment with different study times	Low energy levels	Use short breaks to re-energize

Questions to Answer:

1. **How can you use your strengths to make habit-building easier?**
    - I can seek advice from others who have successful habits and adjust my approach without getting discouraged. I also work well with others, so an accountability partner might help.

2. **What one step will you take to improve on a weakness?**
    - I will focus on breaking down tasks into smaller steps to avoid procrastination and set easier goals to start with.

5.6. Mission 5 Day 6: Creating a Customized Habit Plan

5.6.1. Theory:

Designing a habit plan that fits your unique needs can be a game-changer in achieving your goals. A customized habit plan is not just about picking random activities; it's about creating a roadmap that aligns with your specific profile and aspirations, enhancing your chances of long-term success.

The Importance of a Customized Habit Plan: A customized habit plan is a personal blueprint that adapts to your individual strengths, weaknesses, and goals. Unlike one-size-fits-all strategies, a tailored plan takes into account your unique circumstances and preferences. This personalization ensures that your plan is practical and relevant, making it more likely that you will stick with it over time. Additionally, a flexible plan can evolve with your changing needs and goals, providing ongoing support for your habit formation journey.

Steps to Creating Your Customized Habit Plan:

1. **Set Clear Goals:** Start by defining what you want to achieve. Your goals should be specific and meaningful to you. This clarity helps in selecting the right habits to support these goals.

2. **Choose Your Habits:** Identify habits that align with your goals. For instance, if your goal is to improve fitness, habits might include regular exercise or healthy eating.

3. **Plan Your Routine:** Schedule these habits into your daily life. Consistency is key, so find a time that works for you and stick to it.

4. **Include Rewards:** Build in rewards to reinforce your habits. Positive reinforcement helps maintain motivation and makes the process more enjoyable.

5. **Review and Adjust:** Regularly assess your plan and make necessary adjustments. Life changes, and so might your goals or routines. Flexibility ensures that your plan remains effective and relevant.

Practical Example:

Creating a Study Habit Plan:

Imagine you want to improve your study consistency. Your goal could be to study for 30 minutes daily and review notes Missionly. Plan your study sessions at the same time each day to build a routine. Reward yourself with a favourite activity after studying to reinforce the habit. Periodically review your plan and adjust your study times based on upcoming exams or other commitments.

Why It Matters?

A customized habit plan takes your unique goals, challenges, and lifestyle into account, giving you a roadmap tailored for success. Unlike a one-size-fits-all approach, personalization ensures that your habits align with your needs and motivations. This approach makes it easier to maintain consistency, adapt to setbacks, and celebrate small victories. A well-designed habit plan simplifies decision-making and keeps you focused on progress, helping you build the life you envision with clarity and intention.

Inspiring Thoughts to Reflect On

It is said that,
> "*A clear plan transforms dreams into achievable goals.*"

It highlights the power of strategy in turning aspirations into reality, reflecting a universal approach to success. It is important to have a personal approach, suggesting that alignment with individual strengths brings clarity and direction. Customizing your path ensures you walk it with confidence and purpose. "*The best plans are the ones designed just for you*" reinforces this idea, advocating for a tailored strategy to maximize fulfillment and effectiveness. Together, these quotes advocate for deliberate, personalized planning as essential for confidently navigating life's path.

5.6.2. Mission 5 Day 6 Worksheet:

Objective: Create a detailed plan for implementing and maintaining your new habits.

Instructions:

1. **Set Your Habits:** *Choose three habits you want to focus on. Write them below, along with the cues, routines, and rewards for each habit.*

Habit	Cue (Trigger)	Routine (Action)	Reward (Outcome)

2. **Plan for Consistency:** *Write down how you will stay consistent with each habit (e.g., reminders, habit tracker, accountability partner).*

Habit	Plan for Consistency

Questions to Answer:

1. How will you measure your progress?

   _____

   _____

   _____

   _____

2. What will you do if you miss a day or break the habit chain?

   _____

   _____

   _____

   _____

5.6.3. Sample filled-up Worksheet for a Disciplined Person:

Habit	Cue (Trigger)	Routine (Action)	Reward (Outcome)
Wake up at 5 AM	Alarm clock	Get up immediately	Feeling productive early in the day
Study for 2 hours	Set study time on the calendar	Study without distractions	Knowledge gain and task completion
Exercise for 30 min	Post-study break	Short workout at home	Increased energy and focus

Plan for Consistency:

Habit	Plan for Consistency
Wake up at 5 AM	Use a phone alarm and place the phone far from the bed.
Study for 2 hours	Set specific time blocks on the calendar; use a habit tracker.
Exercise for 30 min	Schedule post-study as non-negotiable; use phone reminders.

Questions to Answer:

1. **How will you measure your progress?**
   - I will measure progress using my habit tracker app, which monitors streaks and completion.

2. **What will you do if you miss a day or break the habit chain?**
   - If I miss a day, I will get back on track immediately the next day, without being too hard on myself, and review what caused the break.

5.6.4. Sample filled-up Worksheet for a Struggling Person:

Habit	Cue (Trigger)	Routine (Action)	Reward (Outcome)
Wake up at 6:30 AM	Alarm clock	Get out of bed immediately	Extra time for morning tasks
Study for 30 min	Phone alarm reminder	Study without distractions	Relief from getting work done
Journal for 5 minutes	Feeling overwhelmed	Write down thoughts and feelings	Mental clarity and stress relief

Plan for Consistency:

Habit	Plan for Consistency
Wake up at 6:30 AM	Set the alarm across the room; create a morning playlist.
Study for 30 min	Use a study app to track progress and reminders.
Journal for 5 minutes	Write for just 5 minutes; reward me with a 10-minute break.

Questions to Answer:

1. **How will you measure your progress?**
   - I will use a habit tracker app to monitor how many days I complete each task and check in Missionly to review my consistency.

2. **What will you do if you miss a day or break the habit chain?**
   - If I miss a day, I won't beat myself up but will get back on track the next day by reviewing what went wrong and adjusting the plan if needed.

5.7. Mission 5 Day 7: Reflection and Next Steps

5.7.1. Theory:

This Mission has been a journey through understanding and refining your habit formation process. By looking back on what you've learned and achieved, you set the stage for continued success in your habit-building journey.

Reflecting on Your Progress: Take a moment to consider the insights you've gained:

- **What have you learned about your unique habit profile?** Reflect on how understanding yourself better has impacted your approach.
- **How have you tailored techniques to fit your personality?** Consider the changes you made to suit your style and their effectiveness.
- **What challenges did you overcome, and how?** Acknowledge the strategies you employed to overcome difficulties.
- **How has your customized habit plan impacted your routine?** Assess how well your plan has integrated into your daily life and its effects.

Celebrating Wins: Recognize and celebrate your achievements:

- **Identify and celebrate the progress you've made in this Mission.** No matter how small, each step forward is a victory.
- **Acknowledge any milestones or small victories**. Celebrate the progress towards your long-term goals.
- **Reflect on how these wins contribute to your long-term goals**. Understand how these achievements fit into your broader journey.

Preparing for Next Mission: Looking ahead:

- **Set new goals based on what you learned during this Mission.** Build on your progress to set clear, actionable goals.
- Adjust your routines and strategies as needed. Fine-tune your plan to improve further.
- **Stay committed to your journey, and keep building on your success.** Use the momentum from this Mission to drive future progress.

5.7.2. Mission 5 Day 7 Worksheet:

Objective: Reflect on your habit journey and plan for long-term success.

1. **Reflection Questions:**

   Q. What did you learn about your habits and personality this Mission?

   _____
   _____
   _____
   _____

   Q. What has been the most helpful strategy in your habit journey so far?

   _____
   _____
   _____
   _____

   Q. How will you continue to personalize and improve your habits moving forward?

   _____
   _____
   _____
   _____

2. **Next Steps:**

Choose one habit you will continue to focus on for the next month. Write down three actions you will take to ensure this habit sticks.

Habit	Actions to take
	1.
	2.
	3.

Questions to Answer:

1. What new habits do you feel confident about maintaining?

   _____

   _____

   _____

   _____

2. How will you keep refining your habit strategies over time?

   _____

   _____

   _____

5.7.3. Sample filled-up Worksheet for a Disciplined Person:

Reflection Questions:

1. **What did you learn about your habits and personality this Mission?**
    - o I learned that my structured approach and self-discipline are strengths, but I need to manage procrastination and low energy better.
2. **What has been the most helpful strategy in your habit journey so far?**
    - o Setting alarms and breaking tasks into smaller, achievable goals have been the most effective strategies.
3. **How will you continue to personalize and improve your habits moving forward?**
    - o I will adjust my toolkit and action plans as I progress, refining habits based on new challenges and strengths I discover.

Next Steps:

Habit	Actions to take
Wake up at 5 AM	1. Place alarm far from bed 2. No phone before bed 3. Consistent sleep schedule

Questions to Answer:
1. **What new habits do you feel confident about maintaining?**
    - o Waking up early and exercising regularly are habits I feel confident in maintaining.
2. **How will you keep refining your habit strategies over time?**
    - o I will continue tracking progress and adjust my tools and routines as I learn more about what works best for me.

5.7.4. Sample filled-up Worksheet for a Struggling Person:

Reflection Questions:
1. **What did you learn about your habits and personality during this Mission?**
    - I learned that I need more external motivation and reminders to keep myself on track and that I tend to overestimate what I can handle in one go.
2. **What has been the most helpful strategy in your habit journey so far?**
    - Breaking tasks into smaller pieces and using reminders like alarms has helped me the most.
3. **How will you continue to personalize and improve your habits moving forward?**
    - I will continue experimenting with different times of the day to see when I'm most productive and adjust my goals to be more achievable.

Next Steps:

Habit	Actions to take
Study for 30 min	1. Set study alarms 2. Use a tracker 3. Break it into 10-min chunks

Questions to Answer:
1. **What is one new habit you want to start next month?**
    - Exercising regularly for 20 minutes in the morning.
2. **How will you make sure you stick to it?**
    - I will use my phone alarm and keep my workout gear ready the night before to minimize effort in the morning.

Chapter – 6

6.1. Mission 6 Day 1: Habit Mastery and Beyond

6.1.1. Theory:

Achieving habit mastery is about transforming your daily routines from basic tasks into second-nature behaviours that drive success. It involves refining and perfecting your habits until they become an effortless part of your life.

What is Habit Mastery? Habit mastery is more than just maintaining good habits; it's about reaching a level where these habits are executed consistently and with high efficiency. It means taking what you've already learned about habits and elevating it to a point where these behaviours feel natural and automatic. Mastery happens when performing your habits becomes so ingrained that it requires minimal conscious effort.

The Benefits of Mastering Your Habits Mastering your habits offers several benefits:

- **Increased Efficiency:** As your habits become second nature, you perform them more efficiently and effectively, freeing up time and mental energy for other tasks.
- **Greater Self-Confidence:** When you consistently practice your habits well, your confidence grows. This self-belief reinforces your ability to tackle more complex challenges.
- **Long-Term Sustainability:** Habits that are mastered are more likely to stick around for the long haul, supporting your long-term goals and contributing to sustained personal growth.

Strategies for Achieving Habit Mastery To reach habit mastery, consider these strategies:

- **Continuous Improvement:** Regularly assess and refine your habits. Look for ways to enhance efficiency and effectiveness.
- **Mindful Practice:** Perform your habits with intention and attention. Focus on each action and its impact.
- **Consistency:** Maintain a steady routine without gaps. Consistent practice is crucial for reinforcing habits.

- **Feedback Loop:** Use data and feedback to track your progress and adjust. Regular reviews help you stay on track and make necessary improvements.

So, achieving habit mastery transforms everyday routines into automatic behaviours that contribute significantly to your success. This process goes beyond merely maintaining good habits; it involves refining them until they seamlessly integrate into your life. The benefits of mastering your habits are profound, including increased efficiency, enhanced self-confidence, and long-term sustainability of positive behaviours. By focusing on continuous improvement, mindful practice, consistency, and creating a feedback loop, you can cultivate habits that become second nature. Ultimately, mastering your habits empowers you to pursue greater challenges and achieve your long-term goals with confidence and ease.

Why It Matters?

Habit mastery is not just about forming new behaviors—it's about transforming your habits into tools for lifelong success. Mastery ensures that positive habits become automatic, freeing mental energy for greater pursuits. By consistently refining your habits, you create a foundation for adaptability, resilience, and continuous growth. Going beyond mastery means leveraging your habits to achieve higher goals, unlocking your true potential, and creating a life of purpose and fulfillment.

Inspiring Thoughts to Reflect On

Aristotle said –

"Excellence is not a singular act, but a habit. You are what you repeatedly do."

It emphasizes that true excellence arises from consistent actions, underscoring his philosophy that habits shape character. Similarly, *"Mastery begins with small steps and grows through relentless consistency"* highlights the idea that sustained dedication and persistence lead to expertise over time. Together, these quotes illustrate that greatness is built incrementally through steady, intentional effort, reinforcing the power of small, consistent actions in achieving mastery.

6.1.2. Mission 6 Day 1 Worksheet:

1. **Define Habit Mastery** in your own words.

   _____

   _____

   _____

2. **List 3 benefits of habit mastery** that you believe will impact your life.

   1. _____

   2. _____

   3. _____

3. **Reflect on one habit** you are currently working on. How can you refine and optimize it?

Questions:

1. What is the process of refining and perfecting your habits called?

   _____

   _____

   _____

2. *Fill in the* blank:

   Habit _____ is about consistently performing at a high level.

3. Why is it important to regularly refine your habits?
   Choose one:
   a) To make life harder
   b) To make habits second nature
   c) To avoid new challenges

Exercises:

1. **Identify one habit** you are trying to master and write down a plan to improve it. Use the following steps:

    o **Refinement:** How can you make it more efficient?

    _____

    _____

    _____

    o **Consistency:** What time can you do it daily?

    _____

    _____

    o **Feedback:** How will you track your progress?

    _____

    _____

    _____

    _____

6.1.3. Sample filled-up Worksheet for a Disciplined Person:

1. **Define Habit Mastery**: Habit mastery is the process of consistently refining and performing habits at an optimal level, making them an integral part of daily life.

2. **3 Benefits of Habit Mastery**:
   - Increases productivity and efficiency
   - Builds long-term success through consistency
   - Reduces decision fatigue by automating positive behaviours

3. **Habit I'm Working On**: I'm currently working on my morning meditation routine. I can optimize it by setting a consistent time each morning and minimizing distractions.

Questions:

1. *Fill in the blank:* Habit **refinement** is about consistently performing at a high level.

2. *Answer:* b) To make habits second nature

Exercises:

1. **Habit**: Morning meditation
   - **Refinement**: Set a specific time (6:30 AM) and reduce distractions by finding a quiet space.
   - **Consistency**: I do it every morning after brushing my teeth.
   - **Feedback**: Track my progress in a journal by noting how I feel after each session.

6.1.4. Sample filled-up Worksheet for a Struggling Person:

1. **Define Habit Mastery**: Habit mastery seems to be about doing habits really well, but I'm not sure I fully understand it yet.

2. **3 Benefits of Habit Mastery**:
   - Helps with being consistent (I think?)
   - It might make life more organized

- I guess it saves time.
3. **Habit I'm Working On**: I've been trying to wake up early, but I keep hitting the snooze button. Maybe I can set multiple alarms or sleep earlier.

Questions:
1. *Fill in the blank:* Habit **refinement** is about consistently performing at a high level.
2. *Answer:* b) To make habits second nature (though I'm not sure what this really means for me)

Exercises:
1. **Habit**: Waking up early
    - **Refinement**: I'm not really sure what I should change to improve. I guess I could go to bed earlier.
    - **Consistency**: I struggle with this, especially when I feel tired.
    - **Feedback**: I haven't really been tracking, but maybe I should start using an app.

6.2. Mission 6 Day 2: Advanced Habit Stacking Techniques

6.2.1. Theory:

Habit stacking is a powerful technique where you attach a new habit to an existing one, creating a seamless chain of actions. By linking habits, you build routines that naturally integrate into your daily life. Advanced habit stacking takes this concept further by incorporating multiple habits into a single, fluid routine. This approach can transform how you manage your time and achieve your goals by leveraging existing habits as a foundation for new ones.

The Power of Habit Stacking

One of the main benefits of habit stacking is increased efficiency. By combining related habits, you streamline your routine, making your daily activities more effective and less time-consuming. Additionally, linking habits strengthens their formation. The repeated association between linked habits reinforces the behaviour, making it easier to maintain over time. When done correctly, advanced habit stacking creates a powerful routine that aligns with your goals and supports your overall success.

Creating an Advanced Habit Stack

To build an effective habit stack, start by identifying a strong anchor habit—the one habit that you already perform consistently and reliably. This habit will serve as the foundation for your stack. Next, add related habits that naturally follow from the anchor habit. Each habit in the stack should have a clear trigger and reward to reinforce its execution. Consistency is key; practice the stack regularly until it becomes an automatic part of your routine.

Practical Example

Consider a morning routine where brushing your teeth is your anchor habit. Build on this by adding:

- Drinking a glass of water immediately afterwards
- Meditating for 5 minutes
- Reviewing your daily goals
- Doing a quick exercise routine

Basically, habit stacking is an effective technique that enhances your daily routines by linking new habits to established ones, creating a seamless flow of actions. This method not only increases efficiency but also reinforces the formation of habits, making them easier to sustain over time. By identifying a reliable anchor habit and carefully selecting related actions to incorporate into your routine, you can create a powerful habit stack that supports your goals. As you practice this advanced approach consistently, you'll find that it transforms how you manage your time, ultimately leading to greater success and a more fulfilling daily life.

Why It Matters?

Advanced habit stacking takes your routines to the next level by strategically linking multiple behaviors. This approach helps you create efficient sequences that reinforce consistency and reduce effort. By mastering these techniques, you maximize productivity and integrate positive habits seamlessly into your daily life. Habit stacking is a powerful way to compound small wins, turning everyday actions into a cumulative force for transformative change.

Inspiring Thoughts to Reflect On

Stacking habits is like building a ladder—each step takes you higher. As someone said –

> *"Success is the result of little things done well over time."*

6.2.2. Mission 6 Day 2 Worksheet:

Instruction: This worksheet helps you to evaluate a current routine of yours and think of ways to improve it.

Worksheet Sections:
1. **Identify a habit** you perform every day that could serve as an "anchor habit."
2. **Create a habit stack** by adding 3 new habits that flow naturally after your anchor habit.

Questions:
1. What does habit stacking involve?
   Fill in the blank: Habit stacking involves linking a new habit to an existing _____.
2. Why is habit stacking effective for building strong routines?
   Choose one:
   a) It saves time by combining habits
   b) It makes habits harder to follow
   c) It complicates your day-to-day tasks

Exercises:
1. **Create your own habit stack** based on your morning routine. Fill in the following table:

Anchor Habit	Habit 1	Habit 2	Habit 3
Example: Brushing teeth	Drink water	Meditate for 5 minutes	Review daily goals

Anchor Habit	Habit 1	Habit 2	Habit 3

6.2.3. Sample filled-up Worksheet for a Disciplined Person:

1. **Anchor Habit**: Brushing my teeth in the morning.
2. **Habit Stack**:
   1. Drink a glass of water
   2. Meditate for 10 minutes
   3. Review my daily goals

Questions:

1. *Fill in the blank:* Habit stacking involves linking a new habit to an existing **routine**.
2. *Answer:* a) It saves time by combining habits

Exercises:

Anchor Habit	Habit 1	Habit 2	Habit 3
Brushing teeth	Drink water	Meditate for 10 minutes	Review daily goals

6.2.4. Sample filled-up Worksheet for a Struggling Person:

1. **Anchor Habit**: I don't have a solid anchor habit. Maybe brushing my teeth?

2. **Habit Stack:**
   1. Wake up early
   2. Drink coffee
   3. Maybe I could try doing a quick workout, but I've never done that before

Questions:

1. *Fill in the blank:* Habit stacking involves linking a new habit to an existing **routine**.

2. *Answer:*

   a) It saves time by combining habits (though I'm not sure how to apply this yet)

Exercises:

Anchor Habit	Habit 1	Habit 2	Habit 3
Brushing teeth	Drink water	Drink coffee	Maybe a 5-minute workout?

For more resources, follow step-by-step:
- Scan the QR-code
- Register/Login Using Email-Id or Phone No.
- Browse through course videos
- Access Feeds for daily motivational & tricks for habit transformation

6.3. Mission 6 Day 3: Building a Resilient Exercise Habit
6.3.1. Theory:

Resilient habits are those that withstand challenges and setbacks, remaining steadfast even when circumstances become tough. These habits are designed to endure through life's unpredictabilities, ensuring that your progress continues despite obstacles. The essence of resilient habits lies in their ability to maintain consistency and effectiveness over time, making them integral to long-term success.

The Importance of Resilience

Life is full of uncertainties, and resilient habits act as a stabilizing force. They help you stay on course, even when faced with unexpected hurdles or disruptions. By incorporating resilience into your habit formation, you build a foundation that supports sustained effort and progress. This resilience ensures that temporary setbacks do not derail your long-term goals, allowing you to recover quickly and continue moving forward.

Strategies for Building Resilient Habits

1. **Start Small:** Begin by establishing small, manageable habits. This gradual approach creates a strong foundation and reduces the risk of overwhelming yourself. Over time, these small habits will accumulate into significant changes.
2. **Stay Flexible:** Adapt your habits as your circumstances change. Flexibility allows you to adjust your routines in response to new

challenges or shifting priorities, ensuring that your habits remain relevant and practical.

3. **Anticipate Challenges:** Plan for potential obstacles and setbacks. By anticipating difficulties, you can develop strategies to overcome them and maintain your habit routine even when faced with adversity.

4. **Seek Support:** Engage with accountability partners or mentors. Support from others can provide motivation, guidance, and encouragement, reinforcing your commitment to maintaining your habits.

Why It Matters?

A resilient exercise habit enhances not just your physical health but also your mental and emotional well-being. Resilience ensures that your commitment to fitness withstands setbacks, busy schedules, or temporary dips in motivation. This habit strengthens your body, boosts your energy, and sharpens your focus, creating a positive ripple effect in all areas of life. Building resilience in your exercise routine sets the tone for consistency and empowers you to take charge of your overall wellness.

Inspiring Thoughts to Reflect On

"Strength doesn't come from what you can do; it comes from overcoming what you once thought you couldn't," says Rikki Rogers, a writer known for her motivational insights that emphasize resilience and personal growth. This quote reflects her focus on the power of persistence, encouraging individuals to redefine their limits and find true strength in overcoming their challenges. Rogers' words inspire a mindset of resilience, urging us to see obstacles as stepping-stones to growth.

6.3.2. Mission 6 Day 3 Worksheet:

Instruction: Think about the rewards you associate with your habits and how they motivate you.

Part 1: Fill in the Blanks

1. Resilient habits are designed to withstand _____ and _____.

2. The essence of resilient habits lies in their ability to maintain _____ and _____ over time.

3. Resilient habits help you stay on course, even when faced with _____ hurdles or _____.

4. Starting with _____, manageable habits helps create a strong foundation for long-term success.

5. _____ your habits as your circumstances change is key to keeping them practical and relevant.

6. Planning for potential _____ allows you to develop strategies to maintain your routine.

7. Support from _____ partners or mentors provides _____, guidance, and encouragement.

Part 2: Exercise – Building Your Resilient Habits
1: Start Small

- Think of a habit you want to build. Write down one small, manageable action you can start with today:

Answer:

_____

_____

_____

_____

2: Stay Flexible

- Reflect on a time when your routine was disrupted by life changes. How could you have adapted your habits to fit the new circumstances?

Answer:
_____

_____

_____

3: Anticipate Challenges

- List two potential challenges you might face when trying to build this habit and how you will overcome them:
    - Challenge 1: _____
        - Solution: _____
          ___
    - Challenge 2: _____
        - Solution: _____

4: Seek Support

- Identify one person who can act as an accountability partner or mentor to help you stay on track with your habit. Why did you choose this person/approach?

Answer:
_____

_____

6.3.3. Sample filled-up Worksheet for a Disciplined Person:

Part 1: Fill in the Blanks

1. Resilient habits are designed to withstand **challenges** and **setbacks**.
2. The essence of resilient habits lies in their ability to maintain **consistency** and **effectiveness** over time.
3. Resilient habits help you stay on course, even when faced with **unexpected** hurdles or **disruptions**.
4. Starting with **small**, manageable habits helps create a strong foundation for long-term success.
5. **Adapting** your habits as your circumstances change is key to keeping them practical and relevant.
6. Planning for potential **obstacles** allows you to develop strategies to maintain your routine.
7. Support from **accountability** partners or mentors provides **motivation**, guidance, and encouragement.

Part 2: Exercise – Building Your Resilient Habits

Question 1: Start Small

- Think of a habit you want to build. Write down one small, manageable action you can start with today:

Answer: I want to build a daily reading habit. I will start by reading 10 pages each morning after breakfast.

Question 2: Stay Flexible

- Reflect on a time when your routine was disrupted by life changes. How could you have adapted your habits to fit the new circumstances?

Answer: During exam season, I didn't have time for long workouts. I could have adapted by switching to 15-minute quick workouts or taking walking breaks to stay active.

Question 3: Anticipate Challenges

- List two potential challenges you might face when trying to build this habit and how you will overcome them:
    - **Challenge 1:** Feeling tired in the morning and skipping reading.
        - **Solution:** I will set out my book the night before to remind myself and make it easier to start.
    - **Challenge 2:** Getting distracted by my phone.
        - **Solution:** I will turn my phone on airplane mode while I read to avoid distractions.

Question 4: Seek Support

- Identify one person who can act as an accountability partner or mentor to help you stay on track with your habit.

Answer: My friend Sarah, who is also working on a reading habit, can help me stay motivated and accountable.

6.3.4. Sample filled-up Worksheet for a Struggling Person:

Part 1: Fill in the Blanks

1. Resilient habits are designed to withstand **challenges** and **setbacks**.
2. The essence of resilient habits lies in their ability to maintain **consistency** and **effectiveness** over time.
3. Resilient habits help you stay on course, even when faced with **unexpected** hurdles or **disruptions**.
4. Starting with **small**, manageable habits helps create a strong foundation for long-term success.
5. **Adapting** your habits as your circumstances change is key to keeping them practical and relevant.
6. Planning for potential **obstacles** allows you to develop strategies to maintain your routine.
7. Support from **accountability** partners or mentors provides **motivation**, guidance, and encouragement.

Part 2: Exercise – Building Your Resilient Habits

Question 1: Start Small

- Think of a habit you want to build. Write down one small, manageable action you can start with today:

Answer: I want to start studying regularly, so I will start by reviewing my notes for 10 minutes after dinner.

Question 2: Stay Flexible

- Reflect on a time when your routine was disrupted by life changes. How could you have adapted your habits to fit the new circumstances?

Answer: I used to stay up late playing video games and couldn't wake up early. I could have limited my game time to adjust my sleep schedule, helping me feel more energized in the morning for schoolwork.

Question 3: Anticipate Challenges

- List two potential challenges you might face when trying to build this habit and how you will overcome them:
  - **Challenge 1:** I might feel too lazy after dinner to start studying.
    - **Solution:** I will remind myself of my goals and set a timer to start studying as soon as I finish eating.
  - **Challenge 2:** My friends might ask me to hang out after dinner.
    - **Solution:** I will let them know I need 10 minutes to study first, then I can join them.

Question 4: Seek Support

- Identify one person who can act as an accountability partner or mentor to help you stay on track with your habit.

Answer: My older brother, who is good at staying organized, can remind me to stick to my plan and keep me focused.

For more resources, follow step-by-step:

- Scan the QR-code
- Register/Login Using Email-Id or Phone No.
- Browse through course videos
- Access Feeds for daily motivational & tricks for habit transformation

6.4. Mission 6 Day 4: Long-Term Habit Sustainability

6.4.1. Theory:

Habit sustainability refers to the ability to maintain habits over an extended period. It's not just about starting a habit; it's about making it a lasting part of your daily life. Sustainable habits integrate seamlessly into your routine, offering ongoing benefits without demanding constant effort or attention. Imagine a tree with deep roots—this symbolizes the strength and permanence of habits that continue to grow and benefit you over the years.

The Importance of Sustainability in Habit Formation

Sustainable habits are crucial for lasting positive change. They ensure that your efforts today will still be effective and beneficial years down the line. Unlike short-lived changes, sustainable habits provide a steady stream of rewards, contributing to your long-term goals without requiring frequent adjustments. This ongoing support makes it easier to maintain motivation and progress, similar to how a well-planned garden thrives with minimal upkeep.

Strategies for Achieving Long-Term Habit Sustainability

To ensure your habits last, integrate them into your identity. When habits become part of who you are, they are more likely to stick. For example, if you see yourself as a healthy eater, making nutritious choices becomes a natural extension of your identity. Also, be prepared to adjust and evolve your habits as life circumstances change. This flexibility helps you adapt without losing momentum. To prevent burnout, pace yourself and allow for occasional breaks or indulgences. Regular reflection and review are essential, helping you tweak and refine your habits to stay aligned with your goals.

Practical Example: Sustaining a Healthy Eating Habit

Consider a habit like healthy eating. Start by identifying as someone who makes nutritious choices, which reinforces your commitment. Adjust your diet as needed based on changes in your health or lifestyle. Allow yourself occasional treats to avoid feeling deprived, which helps maintain balance. Regularly review your meal plans to ensure they continue to meet your needs and preferences.

Why It Matters?

Sustainability ensures that your habits stand the test of time, adapting to changes in your life without losing momentum. By focusing on sustainability, you create routines that are flexible, realistic, and aligned with your long-term goals. This approach prevents burnout and fosters balance, allowing you to maintain progress even during challenging periods. Sustainable habits are the backbone of lasting growth, empowering you to thrive across all stages of life.

Inspiring Thoughts to Reflect On

"Sustainability is not a goal—it's a way of living and growing," reflects a mindset where lasting change is integrated into daily life. As with *"Habits that endure are habits that evolve,"* these words highlight that true sustainability requires adaptability, allowing routines to shift over time. *"Consistency beats intensity when building a life of purpose"* further underscores this message, reminding us that steady, ongoing effort often outpaces brief, intense pushes. Together, these ideas illustrate that building a life of purpose and resilience hinges not on momentary strength but on the quiet power of consistency and adaptability.

6.4.2. Mission 6 Day 4 Worksheet:

Instruction: This can help you learn how tracking can improve consistency and evaluate your current system.

Worksheet Sections:
1. **Identify one habit** that you want to maintain for the next year.

   _____

   _____

2. **Consider how to evolve** this habit as your goals or lifestyle change.

   _____

   _____

Questions:
1. What is habit sustainability?

   Fill in the blank: Habit sustainability is the ability to maintain habits over a long _____.

2. Why is it important to avoid burnout in habit formation?
   Choose one:
   a) So you can keep your energy for other habits
   b) So you can quit the habit when needed
   c) So you can keep the habit going without losing motivation

Exercises:
1. **Plan how to sustain your habit** for the long term:
   - **Integrate into identity:** How can you identify with this habit?

   _____

   _____

- **Adjust and evolve:** What could change in your life that might require an adjustment?

- **Avoid burnout:** How will you pace yourself to stay consistent?

6.4.3. Sample filled-up Worksheet for a Disciplined Person:

1. **Habit to Maintain for a Year**: Exercising 5 days a Mission.
2. **Evolving Habit**: I'll adapt the type of exercise as my fitness goals evolve (e.g., switch from weightlifting to yoga if needed).

Questions:

1. *Fill in the blank:* Habit sustainability is the ability to maintain habits over a long **period**.
2. *Answer:* a) So you can keep your energy for other habits

Exercises:

1. **Sustain My Habit**:
   - **Integrate into identity**: I am someone who prioritizes fitness.
   - **Adjust and evolve**: As I improve, I'll try new forms of exercise (like cycling or hiking).
   - **Avoid burnout**: I'll make sure to include rest days to avoid overexertion.

6.4.4. Sample filled-up Worksheet for a Struggling Person:

1. **Habit to Maintain for a Year**: I want to be able to wake up early consistently, but it feels really overwhelming to think about doing this for a whole year.
2. **Evolving Habit**: Maybe once I get better at waking up early, I could try adding exercise or something productive, but right now, it's hard to think that far ahead.

Questions:

1. *Fill in the blank:* Habit sustainability is the ability to maintain habits over a long **period**.
2. *Answer:* a) So you can keep your energy for other habits

Exercises:

1. **Sustain My Habit**:
    - **Integrate into identity**: I don't really feel like I'm someone who wakes up early. I'm more of a night owl.
    - **Adjust and evolve**: If I could get the hang of waking up early, I might try adding some exercise or something.
    - **Avoid burnout**: I think I'm already feeling burnt out from even trying to change this.

For more resources, follow step-by-step:

- Scan the QR-code
- Register/Login Using Email-Id or Phone No.
- Browse through course videos
- Access Feeds for daily motivational & tricks for habit transformation

6.5. Mission 6 Day 5: Adapting Habits to Life Changes

6.5.1. Theory:

Life is a journey full of twists and turns, and our habits often face challenges as we navigate through it. Adapting habits to life changes is essential for maintaining consistency and achieving long-term success.

Why Adaptability is Key to Habit Success

Habits are not static; they evolve alongside our lives. Major events such as a new job, moving to a new city, or health changes can disrupt established routines. Adaptability is crucial because it allows habits to survive and remain effective despite these disruptions. Habits that can adjust to changing circumstances are more likely to endure and continue to provide value over time.

Common Life Changes That Impact Habits

Several life changes can affect our habits:

- **Major Life Events:** Things like marriage or career shifts can alter daily routines.
- **Health Changes:** Illness or injury may impact physical ability or energy levels.
- **Shifts in Priorities:** New goals or responsibilities can reframe what we prioritize in our routines.
- **Environmental Changes:** Moving to a new location might necessitate adjustments in how we maintain certain habits.

Strategies for Adapting Habits to Life Changes

To ensure your habits remain effective during transitions, consider the following strategies:

1. **Anticipate Changes:** Planning ahead can prepare you for upcoming transitions, making it easier to adjust your habits.
2. **Stay Flexible:** Be open to modifying your habits as necessary to fit new circumstances.
3. **Use Micro-Habits:** Breaking habits into smaller, more manageable steps can help them fit into your new routine.

4. **Focus on Core Habits:** Prioritize habits that are most important to you, ensuring they remain a consistent part of your life.

Why It Matters?

Life is constantly evolving, and so should your habits. Adapting your routines to fit new circumstances ensures that progress continues despite change. This flexibility allows you to stay grounded and focused, even during transitions like a new job, relocation, or personal challenges. By aligning habits with your current reality, you maintain stability while embracing growth. Adaptability is the cornerstone of resilience, ensuring that your habits serve you no matter where life takes you.

Inspiring Thoughts to Reflect On

Albert Einstein said –

"The measure of intelligence is the ability to change."

It highlights that adaptability is a core aspect of true intellect. Similarly, there is such a wisdom in a Chinese proverb,

"When the winds of change blow, adjust your sails,"

It. reinforces this idea by suggesting that resilience lies in our willingness to pivot and embrace new directions. Together, these quotes reflect the powerful truth that growth often requires us to respond flexibly to challenges, adapting to change with an open mind and a readiness to evolve.

6.5.2. Mission 6 Day 5 Worksheet:

Instruction: Use this worksheet to focus on maintaining consistency by building streaks for habits.

1. **List 3 life changes** that could impact your habits in the next year.

   _____

   _____

   _____

2. **Create a plan** for how you'll adapt your current habits to these changes.

   _____

   _____

   _____

Questions:

1. Why is adaptability important for habit success?
   Fill in the blank: Adaptability ensures that your habits survive during _____.

2. Which of the following is a common life change that can impact habits?

   Choose one:

   a) Changes in the environment ☐
   b) Staying at home all the time ☐
   c) Consistently perfect conditions ☐

Exercises:

1. **Pick a habit** that has been disrupted by a recent life change. What strategy will you use to adapt it? Use the steps below:

- **Anticipate changes:** What future changes could impact this habit?

  _____
  _____

- **Stay flexible:** How can you modify the habit to fit new circumstances?

  _____
  _____

- **Focus on core habits:** Which part of the habit is most important to maintain?

  _____
  _____
  _____

6.5.3. Sample filled-up Worksheet for a Disciplined Person:

1. **3 Life Changes**:
    - A new job with different hours
    - Moving to a new city
    - Increased responsibilities at home
2. **Plan to Adapt**: If my job hours change, I'll adjust my exercise routine to fit into my mornings or evenings. I'll also try new forms of exercise that fit my new schedule.

Questions:
1. *Fill in the blank:* Adaptability ensures that your habits survive during **transitions**.
2. *Answer:* a) Changes in the environment

Exercises:
1. **Adapting a Habit**: My reading habit has been disrupted by increased work demands.
    - **Anticipate changes**: My work responsibilities could continue increasing.
    - **Stay flexible**: I'll read in the mornings or listen to audiobooks during my commute.
    - **Focus on core habits**: The core part is reading daily, even if it's just for 5 minutes.

6.5.4. Sample filled-up Worksheet for a Struggling Person:

1. **3 Life Changes**:
    - Increased workload
    - A lot of stress at home
    - Working late hours on a project
2. **Plan to Adapt**: I'm not really sure how to adapt. I guess I could try to sleep earlier, but I always end up working late anyway.

Questions:

1. *Fill in the blank:* Adaptability ensures that your habits survive during **transitions**.

2. *Answer:* a) Changes in the environment

Exercises:

1. **Adapting a Habit**: My goal of waking up early doesn't work well with staying up late for projects or family work. I keep trying, but I'm always exhausted the next day.

    o **Anticipate changes**: I'll probably have more late nights, especially during exam times.

    o **Stay flexible**: I might need to accept that some days I won't be able to wake up early, but I don't want to give up completely.

    o **Focus on core habits**: The core habit is waking up early, but I feel like I'm just not making any progress.

For more resources, follow step-by-step:
- Scan the QR-code
- Register/Login Using Email-Id or Phone No.
- Browse through course videos
- Access Feeds for daily motivational & tricks for habit transformation

6.6. Mission 6 Day 6: Expanding Your Habit Repertoire

6.6.1. Theory:

Expanding your habit repertoire is like nurturing a growing tree; it involves introducing new branches that enhance and enrich your life. By integrating new habits into your routine, you can open doors to personal growth and discover new opportunities.

Why Expand Your Habit Repertoire?

Adding new habits is a powerful way to foster continual improvement and personal development. As you introduce different habits into your life, you create opportunities for growth and progress. This expansion can lead to enhanced well-being and a more fulfilling life. Embracing new habits keeps your routine dynamic and responsive to your evolving needs and interests.

Strategies for Expanding Your Habit Repertoire

1. **Identify Areas for Growth:** Start by considering where you want to improve or what new areas of interest you'd like to explore. Whether it's improving your physical health, learning a new skill, or enhancing your mental well-being, pinpointing these areas helps focus your efforts.

2. **Start Small:** Introduce new habits gradually. Begin with one habit at a time to avoid overwhelming yourself. This approach ensures that you can focus on establishing the new habit without disrupting your existing routine.

3. **Use Existing Habits as Anchors:** Link new habits to established routines. For example, if you already have a daily exercise habit, you could add a new stretching routine that you perform after each workout. This technique helps integrate new habits smoothly into your daily life.

4. **Experiment:** Be open to experimenting with different habits. Trying out various activities or practices helps you find what works best and what enhances your life the most.

Practical Example: Expanding Health Habits

If you have a daily exercise routine, consider adding a new habit like stretching to improve flexibility. Anchor this new habit by doing it right after your workout. Experiment with different stretches to find which ones are most beneficial for you.

Why It Matters?

Expanding your habit repertoire keeps you continuously growing and evolving. By exploring new habits, you push the boundaries of your potential and unlock fresh opportunities for success. This expansion enhances creativity, broadens your skills, and ensures that your personal development journey remains dynamic and fulfilling. Adding new habits to your repertoire also creates a ripple effect, where progress in one area amplifies growth in others. It's a powerful way to sustain momentum and enrich your life.

Inspiring Thoughts to Reflect On

> *"Your potential expands with every habit you master,"*

It speaks to the idea that each small step forward in habit formation propels you toward greater possibilities. Similarly, "The limits of your habits are the limits of your growth" emphasizes that personal progress is directly tied to the habits you cultivate. Together, these insights underline that by building constructive habits, you can unlock new levels of achievement and push beyond self-imposed boundaries, setting the stage for continuous personal growth. So, keep growing. Keep building. Success is found in the stretch.

For more resources, follow step-by-step:

- Scan the QR-code
- Register/Login Using Email-Id or Phone No.
- Browse through course videos
- Access Feeds for daily motivational & tricks for habit transformation

6.6.2. Mission 6 Day 6 Worksheet:

Instruction: This worksheet guides you in learning how to explore Habit Transformation Techniques.

Worksheet Sections:

1. **Choose a habit** you've been working on.
2. **Identify a new technique** (e.g., behavioural substitution, visualization) that could enhance this habit.

Questions:

1. What is behavioural substitution?

   _____

   _____

   _____

2. *Fill in the blank:* Behavioural substitution involves replacing a negative habit with a positive _____.

3. What role does visualization play in habit transformation? *Choose one:*

   a) Helps imagine negative outcomes
   b) Makes the process more complicated
   c) Enhances mental readiness and motivation for habit success

Exercises:

1. **Practice behavioural substitution** for a negative habit you'd like to change.

   Fill in the table given in the next page:

Negative Habit	Positive Substitution	Visualization Strategy
Example: Procrastination	Time blocking	Visualize completing tasks early

6.6.3. Sample filled-up Worksheet for a Disciplined Person:

1. **Habit**: I've been working on reducing social media use.
2. **New Technique**: I'll use behavioural substitution by replacing scrolling with journaling for 5 minutes.

Questions:

1. *Fill in the blank:* Behavioural substitution involves replacing a negative habit with a positive **action**.
2. *Answer:* c) Enhances mental readiness and motivation for habit success

Exercises:

Negative Habit	Positive Substitution	Visualization Strategy
Social media scrolling	Journaling for 5 minutes	Visualize completing my journal entry with focus and clarity

6.6.4. Sample filled-up Worksheet for a Struggling Person:

1. **Habit**: I've been trying to reduce how much time I spend on my phone before bed, but it's really hard to stop.
2. **New Technique**: I'll try replacing phone time with reading a book, but I don't know if I'll actually stick to it.

Questions:

1. *Fill in the blank:* Behavioural substitution involves replacing a negative habit with a positive **action**.
2. *Answer:* c) Enhances mental readiness and motivation for habit success (I don't really feel motivated, though)

Exercises:

Negative Habit	Positive Substitution	Visualization Strategy
Phone use before bed	Reading a book for 5 minutes	Visualize myself putting the phone away, but I haven't been able to do it yet.

For more resources, follow step-by-step:
- Scan the QR-code
- Register/Login Using Email-Id or Phone No.
- Browse through course videos
- Access Feeds for daily motivational & tricks for habit transformation

6.7. Mission 6 Day 7: Reflection and Recap - Habit Mastery Journey

6.7.1. Theory:

As we reach the end of Mission 6, it's time to take a moment to review and reflect on our journey so far. This Mission has been a pivotal point in our Habit Transformation Mastery program, covering essential aspects to enhance and solidify your habits. Let's revisit what we've accomplished and prepare for the next steps in your habit journey.

Reflecting on Your Progress

Take a moment to consider the progress you've made. Reflect on the mastery you've achieved in your habit journey. How have advanced techniques improved your routines? What challenges did you face, and how did you overcome them? Consider how you plan to sustain and expand your habits moving forward. Reflection is crucial as it helps you understand what has worked, what needs adjustment, and how to keep building on your success.

Celebrating Wins

Celebrate the milestones you've reached this Mission. Recognize and appreciate your progress, no matter how small. These wins are not just achievements but stepping-stones towards your long-term goals. Celebrating them keeps you motivated and reinforces your commitment to your habit journey.

Preparing for the Next Mission

As we look ahead, set new goals based on the insights and achievements from this Mission. Adjust your routines and strategies as needed and stay committed to your journey. The skills and knowledge gained in this Mission will serve as a strong foundation for your continued growth.

Key Takeaways

Reflection helps you grasp your progress and challenges, celebrating small wins fuels motivation, and setting clear goals ensures continued success.

6.7.2. Mission 6 Day 7 Worksheet:

Instruction: Review your progress and plan for your ongoing habit journey.

Worksheet Sections:
1. **Reflect on your habit journey** from the past Missions.
2. **Identify your biggest wins** and areas you need to improve.

Questions:
1. What has been your most successful habit transformation so far?

   _____
   _____
   _____

   Fill in the blank: My most successful habit transformation has been _____.

2. How will you continue to refine your habits after this program? *Choose one:*

   a) Quit refining habits
   b) Set new goals for further improvement
   c) Avoid making any changes

Exercises:
1. **Complete a habit reflection** based on your progress:
    - **Biggest habit success:** What habit have you successfully mastered?

   _____
   _____
   _____

- **Area for improvement:** What habit still needs work?

_____
_____
_____
_____
_____
_____

- **Plan for the future:** How will you continue building habits after this course?

_____
_____
_____
_____
_____
_____

6.7.3. Sample filled-up Worksheet for a Disciplined Person:

1. **Reflection on Habit Journey**: My meditation habit has been my biggest success. By creating a consistent routine, I've been able to stay focused and reduce stress.

2. **Biggest Wins**: My morning meditation routine is now a solid part of my day. **Improvement Area**: My reading habit needs more consistency, especially on busy days.

Questions:

1. *Fill in the blank:* My most successful habit transformation has been **morning meditation**.

2. *Answer:* b) Set new goals for further improvement

Exercises:

1. **Habit Reflection**:
    - **Biggest success**: Morning meditation – it's now a non-negotiable part of my routine.
    - **Area for improvement**: Reading habit – I need to find time to read daily, especially when life gets busy.
    - **Plan for the future**: I'll continue to build on my meditation habit by increasing the time to 15 minutes, and I'll refine my reading habit by setting aside time in the mornings for at least 5 pages.

6.7.4. Sample filled-up Worksheet for a Struggling Person:

1. **Reflection on Habit Journey**: I've had a hard time with everything. Waking up early feels impossible, and I still end up on my phone at night. I don't know how to make these habits stick.

2. **Biggest Wins**: I can't really say I've had any big wins yet. **Improvement Area**: Pretty much everything. I need help figuring out how to actually stay consistent.

Questions:

1. *Fill in the blank:* My most successful habit transformation has been **none**.

2. *Answer:* b) Set new goals for further improvement (but I feel like I haven't even achieved the old ones)

Exercises:

1. **Habit Reflection**:

    o **Biggest success**: Honestly, I'm struggling to think of any success.

    o **Area for improvement**: I need to work on everything. I keep losing motivation, and I feel stuck.

    o **Plan for the future**: I'm not sure. Maybe I need to find a way to get back on track, but it's hard to know where to start.

For more resources, follow step-by-step:

- Scan the QR-code
- Register/Login Using Email-Id or Phone No.
- Browse through more resources
- Access Feeds for solving your queries & tricks for habit transformation

Appendix: Additional Resources for Helping Students in Self-study

The resources provided in this appendix are designed to support students in mastering habits, developing self-discipline, and achieving consistent progress. Each tool has been crafted to help you reflect, track, and adjust your actions, making the process of transformation more manageable and effective. Below is an overview of the key templates included in this section:

1. Mission Daily Check-In Template

This template serves as a daily accountability system to help students stay focused and aware of your progress. It prompts you to reflect on your morning, afternoon, and evening activities while also planning for the next day. By answering guided questions, you can overcome obstacles, set implementation intentions, and end your day with gratitude and positivity.

2. Weekly Reflection Summary

Reflecting on your progress after completing a mission or test is critical for improvement. This template helps you analyze your performance, identify areas where you excelled, and recognize the subjects or habits that need more focus. It also encourages you to evaluate your study methods and create an actionable improvement plan for the future.

3. Self-Study Log

Success in habit formation and personal growth relies on consistent effort and self-monitoring. This log enables you to track your study sessions, key topics covered, challenges faced, and your understanding level. By identifying areas where you're struggling, you can take proactive steps to improve and seek support from mentors when necessary.

4. Weekly Productivity Plan

Planning is essential for executing your mission effectively. This schedule allows you to break down your weekly tasks and plan study sessions around your goals. By mapping out your time for each subject or topic, you can ensure steady progress while avoiding last-minute cramming or overwhelm.

Mission Daily Check-In Template

User Name:_____

Date: ____/_____/_____

Goal for the Day:

Day Review (Tentatively at 8 am, 1 pm, 6.45 pm, 9.45 pm, 11-11.30 pm.): (Please feel free to check-in at other timings as per your suitability if these timings do not suit you.)

1. **Morning Reflection at 8 am**:
   - What was your primary focus or intention this morning?

   - Did you accomplish your morning goals? (Yes/No)

   - If no, what challenges did you face?

2. **Mid-Day Check-In at 1 pm**:
   - How did you manage your time and energy till now?

   - Were there any distractions? How did you handle them?

- What did you do well today till now?

3. **Evening Reflection at 6.45 pm:**
    - Did you complete your most important tasks/goal for the afternoon and evening since 1 pm? (Yes/No)

    - What obstacles did you encounter? How did you overcome them?

    - Did you follow through with your planned actions? (Yes/No)

    - How do you feel about your progress till now today?

4. **Mind Contrasting at 9.45 pm**:
    o   What is the most important exam/career related goal you are working towards?

    o   Visualize achieving this goal. How will you feel when you accomplish it?

    o   Identify a potential obstacle that could prevent you from achieving this goal tomorrow.

5. **Implementation Intention during 11 to 11.30 pm**:
    o   State your plan for tomorrow: "If [obstacle] happens, then I will [specific action]."

- o What is the first action you will take tomorrow to move closer to your goal?

6. **Gratitude and Positivity during 11 to 11.30 pm**:
   - o List 3 things you are grateful for today.

   - o End your day with a positive affirmation or thought.

Plan for Tomorrow during 11 to 11.30 pm:

1. **Morning Focus**:
   - o What will be your main focus or intention in the morning?

2. **Key Actions for Tomorrow:**
   o List 3 key actions you will take tomorrow to achieve your goals.

3. **Potential Challenges:**
   o Identify any potential challenges for tomorrow and how you plan to address them.

End-of-Day Summary during 11 to 11.30 pm:

- Overall Satisfaction with Today's Progress (Rate 1-10):
- Any Additional Notes or Reflections:

Signature of Reader:

Accountability Partner's Feedback:
(To be filled by Parents/Teachers/Hostel Wardens)

Signature with Date of Accountability Partner:

Weekly Reflection After a Test/Mission to Improve Next Time

Date:____/_____/_____ Reader Name: _____

This template can be used for weekly reflections on test results and progress. It helps learners identify strengths, weaknesses, and areas to improve.

Reflection Area	Prompt
Initial Reaction and Feelings	Write a brief summary of your immediate reaction to the test results.
Performance Analysis	Subjects/Topics Scored Well and why. Subjects/Topics That Need Improvement.
Specific Mistakes	List mistakes and categorize them: careless errors, conceptual errors, time management issues.
Evaluation of Study Methods	Reflect on the effectiveness of your study strategies.
Improvement Plan	Outline a specific action plan for improvement.

Follow-Up Review Date	Set a date to review your progress.

Weekly Productivity Plan

Reader Name:
Date: ___/___/___   **to Date:** ___/___/___

Time	Monday	Tuesday	Wednesday	Thursday	Friday	Saturday	Sunday
__:__ to __:__	Subject: Chapter: Details:	Subject: Chapter: Details:	Subject: Chapter: Details:	Subject: Chapter: Details:	Subject: Chapter: Details:	Subject: Chapter: Details:	Subject: Chapter: Details:
__:__ to __:__	Subject: Chapter: Details:	Subject: Chapter: Details:	Subject: Chapter: Details:	Subject: Chapter: Details:	Subject: Chapter: Details:	Subject: Chapter: Details:	Subject: Chapter: Details:
__:__ to __:__	Subject: Chapter: Details:	Subject: Chapter: Details:	Subject: Chapter: Details:	Subject: Chapter: Details:	Subject: Chapter: Details:	Subject: Chapter: Details:	Subject: Chapter: Details:
__:__ to __:__	Subject: Chapter: Details:	Subject: Chapter: Details:	Subject: Chapter: Details:	Subject: Chapter: Details:	Subject: Chapter: Details:	Subject: Chapter: Details:	Subject: Chapter: Details:
__:__ to __:__	Subject: Chapter: Details:	Subject: Chapter: Details:	Subject: Chapter: Details:	Subject: Chapter: Details:	Subject: Chapter: Details:	Subject: Chapter: Details:	Subject: Chapter: Details:
__:__ to __:__	Subject: Chapter: Details:	Subject: Chapter: Details:	Subject: Chapter: Details:	Subject: Chapter: Details:	Subject: Chapter: Details:	Subject: Chapter: Details:	Subject: Chapter: Details:
__:__ to __:__	Subject: Chapter: Details:	Subject: Chapter: Details:	Subject: Chapter: Details:	Subject: Chapter: Details:	Subject: Chapter: Details:	Subject: Chapter: Details:	Subject: Chapter: Details:

Daily Habit Tracker

Reader Name:_____

Date	Subject / Topic Studied	Study Session Duration (Start - End Time)	Key Concepts Covered	Level of Understanding (1-5)	Challenges Faced / Areas of Struggle	Actions to Improve / Next Steps	Mentor Feedback